Following Claire

Jenny Jeffries
PO Box 45299
Te Atatu
Auckland
New Zealand

ISBN-13: 978-1517407582

https://followingclaire.wordpress.com/
www.facebook.com/outrageousoutlander
Twitter: @sniskybobfry

Visit www.jennyjeffries.nz to contact the author and see other
examples of her work

Following Claire
by
Jenny Jeffries

Introduction

Anyone who hasn't read 'Outlander' by Diana Gabaldon, or seen the series currently being filmed by STARZ, will wonder who on earth the Claire mentioned in the title of this story is.

Claire is the protagonist of the Outlander books – it is from her viewpoint that we discover what it was like to fall back through the stones from 1945 to 1743. Those of us who already loved Scotland, were easily enthralled by the setting, and became enamoured with the main characters and especially James Alexander Malcolm McKenzie Fraser, or Jamie, a highlander whom Claire falls in love with.

The series first started showing in New Zealand midway through 2014, and the previews had me hooked from the start. Being a graphic designer and cartoonist, with a sturdy sense

"Nay, Jamie, dinna leave me! Claire? Claire? Think o' Frank"

STARZ

+ @sniskybobfry

of humour, I took the liberty of 'insinuating' myself into some of the scenes STARZ tempted us with, imagining how ludicrous it would be for myself to be sent back there in time. This proved to be such a hit on Facebook and Twitter that I set up my Outrageous Outlander page and have not exhausted all the possibilities inherent in incorporating myself in the show yet. What followed of course, was heightened interest in Scotland, and in particular, the places where the filming had happened. Many of the historic sites and old villages in Scotland still retain a strong link to their past and have been preserved to retain their original character, which makes filming scenes from the 1800s much easier I am sure.

When I heard that the fans in the United Kingdom were planning a major gathering to be held in Crieff over a long weekend in May 2015, initially I just felt a little jealous. But my own plans to visit Scotland later in the year changed, and I was able to take the place of someone who had pulled out of the UK Outlander Gathering, and be the only representative from New Zealand attending. Naturally, I planned to see Scotland while I was there, and this time, for at least a month.

I have visited Scotland twice in my past: the first time with a friend and carrying a heavy backpack, using public transport and hostels, back in 1989. The second time more recently, in a whirlwind week in the Highlands by minibus in the winter. This was through Haggis Tours, and in December 2012, with a crowd of much younger people, but I realised afresh that I needed to return and take much longer to see it all.

My return in May 2015 was for a month, driving myself around in a rented car, and just having a rough idea of where I would like to go. Primarily, I would be keeping an eye out for Outlander film sites and meeting up with Outlander fans whom I would meet at The Gathering. For this reason, I called my trip, 'Following Claire'. I made up a 'bucket list' of points I would like to achieve on my trip, which are outlined in the next pages. Most of these I did, and many more not written there, and the ones I did not get to do were not for want of trying.

I believe I can honestly say that every single day of my trip around Scotland and the Highlands was a rich and delightful experience, unlike any holiday I have had before. For that reason alone I felt it worthwhile writing down my day-by-day journey with accompanying pictures, just in case there were any who want to 'follow Jenny' as she is 'Following Claire'. I do hope you enjoy the experience too.

Finally, this illustrated narrative is not intended to be a dissertation on Scotland, but a whimsical account of my impressions as I drove around. I feel sure that many times I made errors in my conclusions about where I was, or how old the houses or buildings are, or who actually built the castle, or even what a broch was for. If you are of a scholarly turn of mind, you may cringe at the revelation of my inept research and quite rightly too! I ask you to put yourself into the seat beside me, in the little VW polo, and just go for the ride. It won't be polished, and will be beset with some false impressions, but on the whole, was a lot of fun. When you feel you cannot bear any more, reach down beside you to the silver hip flask and take a sip of that good Scottish whisky. Relax. Someone else has written more accurately about those things you are fretting over.

* * *

I would sincerely like to thank a whole list of people who came with me emotionally, mentally, and online, even though they were not physically there with me. I never felt truly alone in all my days related in the following pages, and it is due to these folk who made that possible. I am almost afraid to start the list for fear of leaving anyone out, but here goes:

My mother, from whom the Urquhart side of the family

comes, ever a supporter of all that I do. My sister, Helen, who truly knows me and has always be there for me, and her daughter and my niece, Jemma, also a keen fan of the books. A singular group of Outlander fans I have met relatively recently in my life, but with whom I regularly interact. Some of these I took in the form of 'pockets' to Scotland with me, laminated cardboard cutouts of them stuck in the side pockets of the car, in my suitcase, or occasionally in a photo at a landmark. One of these, Rhonnie Brinsdon, from New Zealand, had made me the outfit which I wore at The Gathering and which features in the Scottish newspaper article. She is even now designing my French collection for the coming Series of Outlander. Karen Brand, probably my first fan on Facebook and Twitter for

the Outrageous Outlander memes, and still faithfully supporting me from Michigan, USA. Annie Featherstone, from NZ, with whom I have coffee often, who encourages me in all my efforts in writing and travelling. Other 'memers' who I play with online – Bridgette (@brigitte_jean) who came across from Germany to the Netherlands, just so we could actually meet up, and Nancy (@Veilsrus) from North Carolina. Phil and Jean Macomber, from Jacksonville, Florida, who opened their home to a stranger (me) so I could see the Outlander series when it first started. All of the others that get a mention in the story, because of their generosity and

Outlander passion, but particularly Fiona Potter, who went above and beyond the call of duty to show me around both Edinburgh and Glasgow. And of course, the Kiwi Outlander fans on Facebook, and the ANZOFs, the Australian and New Zealand fans, both of whom were fully behind my trip and delivery of card, presents and invitation to Sam Heughan and Caitriona Balfe. (We still hope to see them Downunder in the near future).

I want to take a special moment to thank Diana Gabaldon, without whose inspiration my trip to Scotland would have been unpeopled by the characters I've come to love. And also Ron Moore, Terry Dresbach and team, who tirelessly work to bring those characters to life on the screen. Thank you so much!

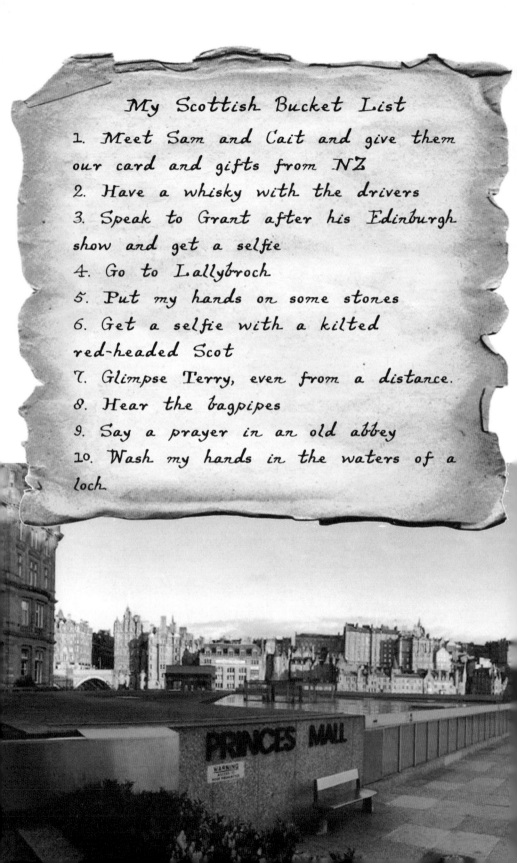

My Scottish Bucket List

1. Meet Sam and Cait and give them our card and gifts from NZ
2. Have a whisky with the drivers
3. Speak to Grant after his Edinburgh show and get a selfie
4. Go to Lallybroch
5. Put my hands on some stones
6. Get a selfie with a kilted red-headed Scot
7. Glimpse Terry, even from a distance.
8. Hear the bagpipes
9. Say a prayer in an old abbey
10. Wash my hands in the waters of a loch

11. Walk in George Square, Glasgow
12. Ride a bike around some remote wilderness
13. Stand on the shores of a beach in the west, with my feet in the sea.
14. Climb up a peak and take a deep breath.
15. Finger some homespun fabric
16. Eat some fish from the north sea
17. Walk up the winding stairs of a turret tower
18. Let the memory of lives lost at Culloden give me pause.
19. Smell the crisp scent of the highlands
20. Dance until my feet hurt.

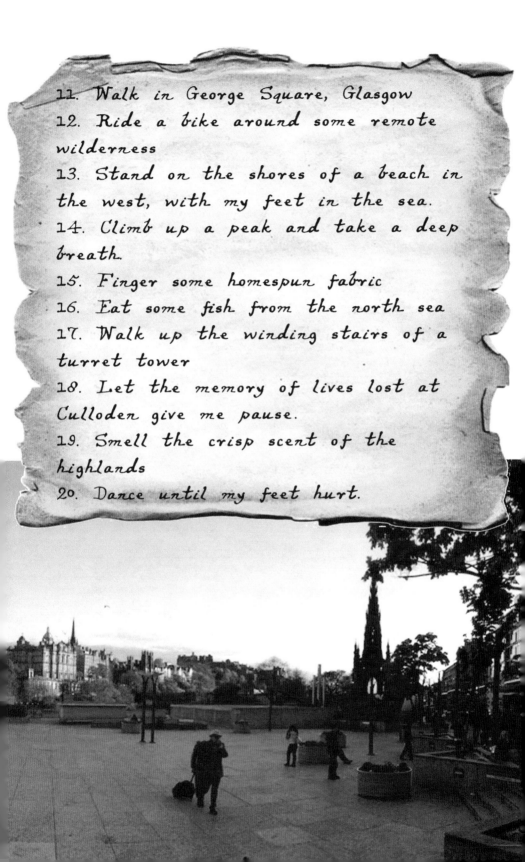

Monday 11 May

Auckland through Shanghai and Paris to Edinburgh

If you were to push a needle through the centre of the earth from Auckland, the sharp end would push through into the Royal Mile in Edinburgh, probably in the pub called 'The World's End'. The name of that pub could not be more appropriate given the journey across to Scotland from New Zealand. No matter which way you go, (and believe me, I've tried most of them), it still takes the better part of 25 hours of flying time and casts you shivering into a climate the opposite of the one you just left.

Wooed by the prospect of a considerably cheaper flight, I decided to try the new flight path that Air New Zealand is now taking via China. Sadly, the Air New Zealand portion of the flight ends there in Shanghai, and after twelve and a half hours of uncomfortable economy class, and little sleep, you must negotiate customs and remove your baggage to begin again with a new airline. (Some problem with Kiwi and Chinese baggage handlers has meant they will not handle each other's bags!)

Anyway, the first leg of my journey was as pleasant as it could be, in an exit row I had paid a further $100 for, so that my legs were able to enjoy unprecedented room, at a cost to my hips and upper body, which had to fit a slightly narrower seat, and share an intimacy over the armrest with the passenger to my direct right. Fortunately, he proved a friendly and placid American-living-in-New Zealand, who did not want to discuss every aspect of my trip, or his, with me. Instead we both shared pleasantries before settling into the acrobatic task of eating over the tiny unfolding table that – along with the computer screen – can be drawn out of the armrest. That explained the narrowness of our seats!

Arriving in Shanghai at noon the plane descended through

the haze of brown smog and then negotiated a series of runways, finally coming to a halt out in the middle of the tarmac. Other similarly displaced planes waited, and we ourselves were herded out down the stairs to await the bus. It was like all my remembered visions of public transport in China. Squeezing with bag into the bus until there was no more room, and when you thought you could squeeze no more people in, even more bodies were eased on until it was unnecessary to use the dangling handles, because you were so wedged against the crush.

Actually, customs in Shanghai was not as bad as I had experienced it in Los Angeles. With blank-faced efficiency, I was progressed through the monitors and checks, recovered my suitcase, and soon found the terminal from which Air France would carry me off to Paris. Not that I rushed. For some reason I was under the delusion I had about four hours in Shanghai, and I did not check my itinerary. Having no Chinese currency neither did I stop for coffee or purchases, but instead ambled around the terminal area looking at the interesting Asian products on display. I even lay down along some seats for a blissful half an hour stretching out my back. It wasn't until a heavily French-accented voice penetrated my consciousness with the words: "Final boarding call for Air France flight 117 for Paris" that I sprang forward to the Gate to find I was almost the last passenger.

On this particular leg of my journey I enjoyed the illusion I was going to Paris listening to flight staff speaking with French accents. I had paid extra for the 'economy comfort' seat as well, which turned out to be one which faced the wall leading into business class: a mixed blessing. On the one hand, my knees were not butting the back of the seat in front, and my legs ALMOST able to stretch out completely (the space fell about 10 centimetres short of that). On the other hand, for periods of time the curtains were open into business class, and I had the luxury of watching how much more spacious and accommodating that area actually was. I could see how delighted the passengers there were with their champagne; how relaxed they seemed as their seats inclined back until almost fully prone. But that is being picky.

The French flight attendant 'working' our side of the section discovered my nationality, and his face brightened. Whenever he passed by, he stopped to ask another question or comment. It cannot have been because I looked at all alluring! If I was under that illusion it was shattered upon my first trip to the restroom, where the glare of the light in that tiny space caught every puffy-eyed, fluffy-haired close up of a face that's been in transit too long. He must have just been expressing the French male's natural charm.

It was he who introduced me to cognac with coffee, bless him. When he found I preferred one to the other (yes, he gave me two), he popped another bottle of my preference in my lap on his next round. Somewhat lighter-headed and looser in limb, I disembarked at Charles de Gaulle airport, and made my way to the next terminal, where Air France would take me to Edinburgh. I saw nothing of Paris. . . and in my present state, did not care.

Paris to Edinburgh took only one hour forty-five minutes, but they were the longest minutes yet, on this journey. You cannot appreciate how stiff you feel, how utterly tired and puffy and sticky and disorientated you are until you have done a trip like this without overnight stopovers. And even though I have regularly told myself I will include them, the reality is that when weighed against what you might use that money for later, spending a chunk of it to sleep in a hotel bed on the way seems excessive.

It was 9.30 at night when that plane touched down but it was still quite light outside and my heart had become equally light as well; positively buoyant in fact. I was finally, at last, back in Scotland! There was the Forth Bridge. There the North Sea and the coastline I loved. The airport sign welcoming me to Edinburgh seemed to have been set up just for me. Still grinning I rolled my purple bag for the last time up the tunnel between plane and terminal and overheard the burr of the Scottish accent in voices around me. Oh Joy!

The next hour or so was a blur of squeaking baggage rotundas, laden trolleys, and then the blast of cold air as I went outside to find the bus to the city. Wait – cold air? Wasn't it summer in Scotland? It felt a bit winterish to me, and colder than the air in Auckland I had left a couple of days ago, and New Zealand was sliding into winter. With confidence borne from having been here only two and half years earlier, I went outside to the bus stop and was soon being driven into the main rail terminal in the heart of the city. From there, my B&B was a short few blocks away.

The guesthouse I had booked online from the comfort of my office in Te Atatu, was one called York House, and situated at 27 York Place, in New Town just outside the older city. It had cost £90 for two nights, for a small room and sharing a bathroom on the first floor. There was only one other room occupied but such was my delight at finally reaching my destination and a bed that it felt palatial.

Tuesday 12 May – Wednesday 13 May, Edinburgh

I woke at 4am to find light streaming in through the only window and the sound of moving traffic outside my window. This booking did not include breakfast, but I was keen to get out and have a proper Scottish breakfast at a cafe of my choosing, and by 7.30 was striding purposefully up toward the old city and 'The Mile'.

My face wore a grin for most of my month around Scotland, and this is where that grin took hold. Striding confidently past the entrance to the railway station, I walked up the steep and winding Cockburn Street, with its cobblestones and quaintly old buildings, past the hostel I had stayed in two and a half years earlier. There near the top was the 'Southern Cross Café', full of hints of my homeland inside, and where  (I believe) the owner is a New Zealander. Perfect! Casting my mind back, I remember regaling the poor Scotsman behind the counter with details of my nationality and upcoming adventure, and asking for a "Full Scottish breakfast please – yes, WITH the haggis"! He looked amused and probably rolled his eyes when his back was turned.

Out came a sturdy 'flat white', (What? Our flat whites are served here now?), followed by a plate weighed down with sausages, haggis, bacon, tomatoes, potato rosti, eggs, and black pudding. Here, at the start of my trip, that breakfast was a miracle of flavours and substance, the like of which I had not tasted. Let me add that

as the weeks progressed and each breakfast I had after that in a B&B was a 'Scottish one', the appeal of that line up of items began to wane by Week Two. (By Week Four I was munching toast and eggs.)

Bolstered up by that repast, I walked next door to a newsagency to purchase a UK sim card, intending to use my I-phone's GPS application for navigating the roads. What seemed a simple transaction proved more difficult than it should have been. The somewhat disinterested salesperson behind the counter took out a Vodafone sim and had installed it and changed my phone settings when his boss arrived from across the street, where he ran a pizza place(!). Upon learning that Vodafone had been installed on my phone, he threw up his hands in horror and said that would not do. He took out the newly installed card, and finding a Lebara sim card, installed that instead, informing me as he did so, that I would find them more useful for global roaming.

I thanked him heartily and set off up the Mile toward Edinburgh castle.

Now, in saying that last sentence in one line like that, I doubt you get the full sensory pleasure I was experiencing with every step I took and every sweet thrill of knowledge that danced through me at where I was. I was back in Edinburgh, walking up a cobbled street, with 'Closes' and ancient brick or stone buildings on either side, and a distant sound of bagpipes ahead. True, the air was nippy and the wind tugged at my coat, but I could not have been happier. The grey granite of Edinburgh with the many higgledy-piggledy chimneys, the ancient buildings, and the narrow winding hill of rough cobbles, monuments, clock towers and swinging signs.

Right where I expected it to be, the gates of Edinburgh castle opened up, and I was swept in with a small crowd of tourists like a boat bobbling along in a river. Here I wanted to pick up my 'Scottish Explorer Pass', purchased online in New Zealand, where the application required I specify a pick up place. Unfortunately, when I found the office, it was to discover that from the moment I picked up my Pass, it would be stamped and my two weeks of usage begin.

Now I was heading off to the UK Outlander Gathering in a day or two for four days, and by the time I could actually start to use the Pass, it would be a week into its two-week window. There was nothing that could be done about it, but the nice woman who stamped my Pass wrote a note on it asking that it be started a week later. (Not something the system would allow, as it turns out). In retrospect, and as advice for any reading this, I would not bother with a Scottish Explorer Pass unless you are intending to rush around from castle to castle using it straight away. Good luck with that.

By now I had sent a text on my new UK number to a local Outlander I had only met on Twitter, who had agreed to meet me outside 'The Real Mary King's Close' further down the Mile. Fiona Potter, a sprightly blonde with her tidily ponytailed hair (and carrying a large plastic bag that later turned out to be a gift for me), recognised me first and we laughed and hugged each other. It was to be the first of some wonderful meetings with fans I had only tweeted with or posted with on Facebook.

After we recovered from the excitement of meeting each other offline, Fiona and I headed down The Mile (High Street) toward Holyrood Palace at the very bottom. Back in the 16th century, the king travelled between the Castle at the top and the

Palace at the bottom, and so it was nicknamed 'The Royal Mile'. I'm sure it meant nothing to him to move back and forth between the two places, carried as he was by various carriages or minions, but it IS a hill and for me, newly arrived yesterday and wearing shoes that needed breaking in, it was good exercise. Fiona, of course, bounced jauntily along at my side, chatting merrily whether she was going uphill or down. On the left side we passed a silversmith's (http://www.hamiltonandyoung.co.uk/) window, and Fiona said that they featured specifically made Outlander items. I was thrilled to discover more than just a token nod at Outlander inside: there was a full-sized Jamie standee! Naturally, we posed for photos and I bought my first souvenir from Scotland in this shop; a silver-plated Clan Fraser whisky flask for £20.

Onward and downward we walked, until High St turned into Canongate (still part of the Mile) and a distant skirl of pipes could be heard growing ever louder. Through the colossal gates of Holyrood Palace a flash of kilts and coats on parade! This is the Queen's official Edinburgh residence. We joined a small throng all  snapping photos of what turned out to be the last moments of a parade of soldiers and cadets, marching to the pipes. It was obvious we were not going to get inside for a look around just yet, so we looked at our options. Fiona had paid for tickets to The Real Mary King's Close, back at our starting point, and we realised we would need to start back up the hill to get there in time.

The entrance to this 'exhibition' could easily be passed by. There is so much to see and so many similar posters and tours, that this entrance just a short way up from Cockburn St on the right, is one among many. I had read about it though, and heard that it was an excellent tour under old Edinburgh, a labyrinth of passages and rooms, all preserved from the 16oos when it was the central business district. The Royal Exchange was eventually built over the area, and rather than tear the bottom levels down, the new building rose over the old, burying it until it was excavated in recent day. After entering through the shop, we joined a group led by our garrulous guide down a long stairway into the depths. I did not really believe our guide when he said it was a place you could get lost in, until we had trailed through two 'houses' across a corridor and into yet another set of ancient rooms. Here was evidence of an early dwelling with fire pit and peeling plaster and worn floorboards. Even knowing that 'back in the day' the sky was somewhere a few flights overhead, real sunlight can never have pierced the dim interiors in which these people pursued their short lives. Or so it seemed to me. We heard many stories along the way, and indeed, some of the stories were well supported by real mannekins and furniture. The best moment came upon stepping out into what had been the main thoroughfare: a steep narrow street where wares had been displayed, chamber pots emptied overhead, and the clatter of carts, dogs and horses. This was the place where trade had been carried out, and a workshop or two was still evident. (Maybe even a ghost, according to the popular rumour.) Fiona and I had our photo taken beneath dangling laundry, on an infrared camera, so that we looked a bit ghoulish ourselves.

We finally ascended into the light, pleased with the whole experience, but ready to sit and chat over lunch. The main event we were both looking forward to was happening at 2pm down at the Lyceum theatre (www.lyceum.org.uk) on Grindlay Street, just past Grassmarket. Grant O'Rourke, who plays Rupert in Outlander,

1. Apologies right now to all who were disappointed that I did not immediately remember them. Often I would get back to my room and the penny dropped then. I know who you are on Twitter, truly!

was appearing in the title position in the comedy, 'The Venetian Twins', and we had front row seats for the matinee. Not only that, but a group of Outlander fans from the USA and UK were also attending and it would be a lively meeting beforehand. The chance of actually meeting one of the actors from Outlander had me all aquiver, and in my bag was a humble offering I was prepared to lay at his feet: a small photobook of my OutrageousOutlander memes. I had my I-pad, I-phone and camera, in hopes that a photo with him might also be in the offing.

By 1.30pm Fiona and I were outside the theatre, a cool breeze flapping the billboard up in the corners, and a small crowd gathering in clustered groups. So began what was a pattern for my encounters with Outlander fans over the course of the next week. I already stand a head taller than many people, but with my corseted and sturdy frame in almost every meme I have put up on Twitter and Facebook, and my long blonde plait, no-one fails to recognise me. I, on the other hand, know people more by their twitter handle or the tiny image they choose to be depicted as, and few use their own faces. The conversation usually starts by someone in the distance exclaiming loudly: "Oh, look, it's sniskybobfry!" I respond with a hearty "Hello!!" – hugs or excited babbling all around. [1]Various ones introduced themselves to me, but my brain being the sieve that it is, no sooner has the name bobbled around in there for a minute than it has been overtaken by the next person's and so on and so on. It WAS lovely to be in a crowd of 'my people' though, and I got to meet Tricia, an admin from Florida, who had kindly taken a [2]Pocket Jenny with her to San Diego last year and got a signature from Caitriona Balfe on the back for me. At some point in the coming week I was reunited with my 'pocket' and little Jenny is with all the other pockets back in my studio.

The excitement was palpable as the first few rows in front of the stage filled, and it became apparent that many were Outlanders. We stood and greeted each other, we laughed, we took photos, we

2. Outlander Starz produced some printed glossy card Jamie and Claire 'pockets' (and other characters) to market the show to fans. Pocket Jenny is a handmade replica of myself in cardboard.

whispered and waited. At Grant's first entrance on the stage, I am sure a flurry of movement and soft cheer greeted him, and he displayed remarkable concentration NOT to be put off his stride.

It was a hilarious comedy show – lots of mistaken identity, comic timing, desperate bravado, and above all, fast costume changes, and we all loved it. This was 'Rupert' as we had never seen him. After the curtain went down we gathered nervously out in the entrance, hoping he would join us, all clutching our programmes, a pen, cameras, and talking excitedly, eyes darting to and fro. By the time he joined us, my hitherto relaxed and jolly demeanour had given way to a flushed, perspiring, gabbling, parody of myself, but he kindly allowed me to kiss his cheek and thrust my Outrageous Outlander booklet into his hand. The photos say it all, and there were a few of them. In all of them Grant looks a little wary. Sigh. Somehow I came away from that encounter with a signed playbill, some digital photos, and an uncomfortable awareness I had lost sight of my immediate surroundings for a while along with my dignity. Still, I'm very pleased with the photo I have of kissing his cheek, which can go beside the one I have kissing Graham McTavish's cheek in Hamilton.

The theme of a 'comedy of errors' continued, spilling over into real life for a moment. My phone was not working properly. No access to the internet. Fiona faithfully stayed by my side and the others headed off for refreshments with a loose arrangement for us all to meet up for drinks and food. I was to text them when I had sorted out my phone issue. The two of us stumbled uphill toward the Mile, chatting about the show, and feeling colder and more tired by the minute. Quite suddenly we stopped and turned around: "Why are we doing this? I'll sort the jolly phone out on my way home, let's go find the girls!"

We couldn't get hold of them by phone, so we searched most of the places that served food and drink in the vicinity of the theatre, and there were MANY. Somehow Fiona got hold of someone, who said they were all at Greyfriar's Bobby's Bar, a restaurant and bar on the other side of Grassmarket. And so we found ourselves clustered around a round table enjoying a dish of Cullen Skink, and reminiscing about Outlander and the coming Gathering. The photos all show me glazed-eyed and rosy-cheeked and grinning stupidly at the camera.

When I farewelled Fiona she handed me the huge bag she had been carrying all day, and in it was a metal thermos flask, a tin of shortbread, and my various purchases she had carried because my own bag was so small! The flask was a gift she had offered to buy me when we talked online before I came – I thought she meant a water flask for the car, and so suggested a large one, given the choice. She meant a thermos flask, for tea and coffee, and had lugged this superb stainless steel receptacle around all day. THAT is the calibre of person I was lucky enough to count as friend!

At the top of Cockburn Street I went in to the Newsagent that had sold me the useless Sim card and found the owner there. He took my phone off me and discovered he had forgotten to adjust the passcode and other Lebara details in the settings, and

having done so, handed it back, working perfectly. [NOTE: the Sim card ceased to be of any use once I hit the Highlands, and did not find the internet again until I returned to Glasgow. Fortunately, all the roads in the Highlands are one-lane and go to the main centres without the need for GPS, but it made booking accommodation online an impossibility].

Arriving back at York House, it was only when I eased my shoes off that I discovered a blister under one foot where the inside of my shoe had been a bit rough. It was certainly no surprise – I crested the hill that Edinburgh castle sits on a number of times during the day, and a certain numbness had set in. I gingerly put a plaster on it, and fell gratefully into my narrow bed.

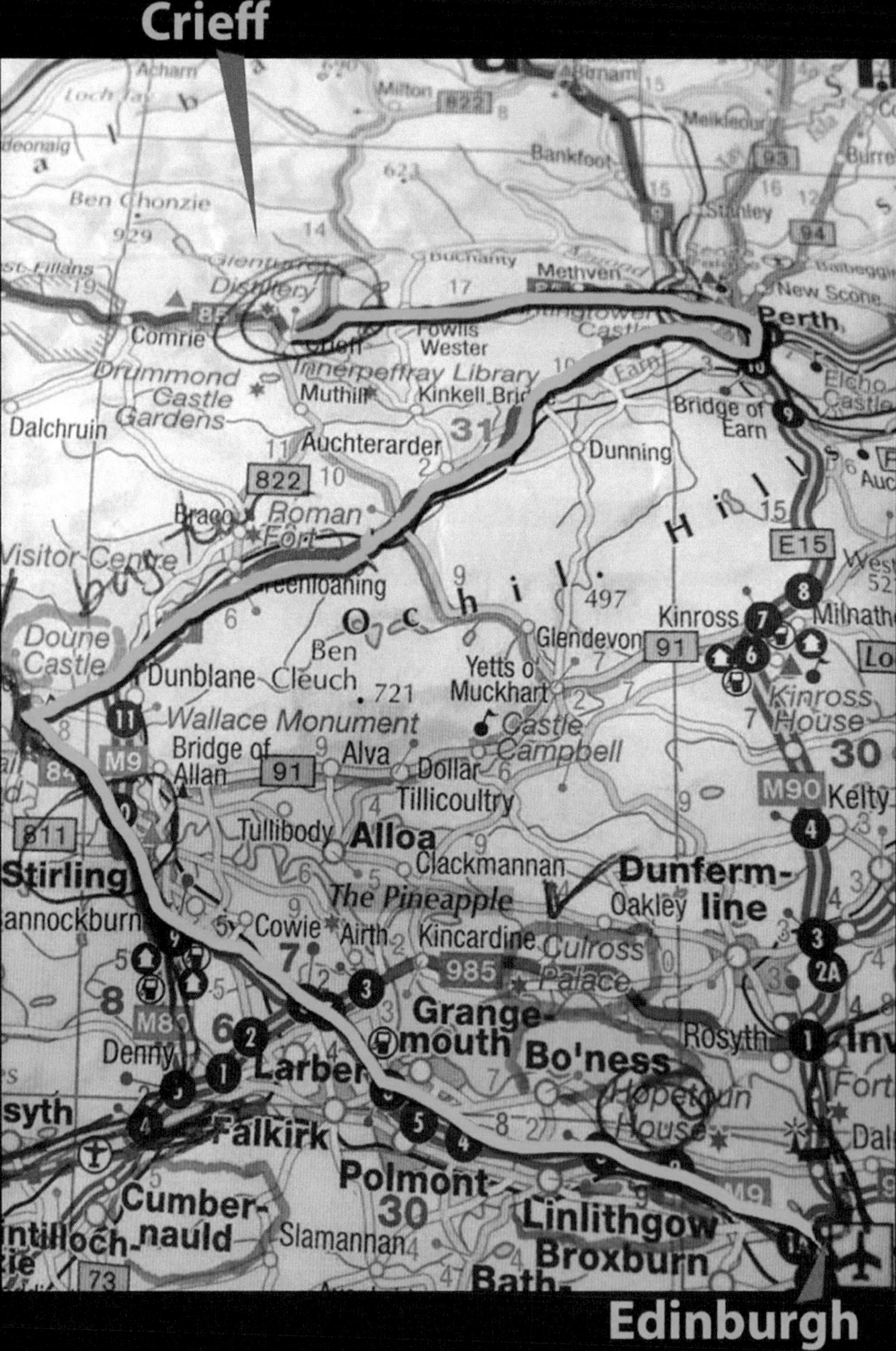

Thursday 14 May
Edinburgh to Crieff

I got up in a leisurely fashion, having been woken again at 4am by light filtering in through the window and an increase in traffic noise. Today I needed to get up to Crieff by mid-afternoon, where I hoped to settle in to my B&B and then go and meet Outlanders at the [3]Gathering in the evening.

I gathered my possessions into the two receptacles I had brought: a medium wheelie bag emblazoned with the 'Outrageous Outlander' logo on both sides, and a smaller purple wheelie, and proceeded to get them both downstairs. (This was to become something so arduous on the first two weeks of my travels, that eventually I took to putting just a change of underwear and bathroom essentials into the purple bag and using the car boot/ trunk as a 'tallboy').

The air was crisp and breezy and I wore my puffer jacket. I was beginning to realise that the transition from winter in New Zealand to late spring in Scotland was going to be very smooth. In fact, I was to wear my small selection of winter clothes in tight rotation for the next month, but on this second day, I did not know that.

The railway station was a few blocks away, and I passed a few travelers like me, whose suitcases were kicking up a din over the cobbles and cracks in the pavement. So immersed was I in the surroundings and the need to reach the right terminal that I was completely taken by surprise when a voice rang out from the pavement ahead: "Jenny!" Bear in mind, I knew NO-ONE in Edinburgh, for Fiona had left for her own home the day before. Even as I focussed on the eager face

3. 2015 UK Outlander Gathering held at the Crieff Hydro Spa

drawing closer, I registered the American accent, and by the time I was enveloped in a hug had realised I was being greeted by an [4]Outlander. It was Susan W, a cheery blond from USA, who had recognised me from my 'Outrageous Outlander' memes! I really enjoyed that friendly, if brief, hello – and we both discussed our coming weekend at Crieff and our excitement at being in Scotland.

I had paid online for my rail trip from Edinburgh to Perth, and had an hour to wait until departure at 10:03. A nearby fast-food restaurant in the terminal had wifi and space to park my bags and coats, and that was where I breakfasted on this second day.

Soon I was rolling along on rails in a comfy window seat, watching Edinburgh slip away and the green countryside leading west toward Stirling sweep past my window. It was remarkably like the Waikato in New Zealand, south of the Bombay hills, with pastures dotted with cows, and rolling hills. I saw the promontory from which Stirling castle commands so amazing a view, enabling it to hold such an important position in Scottish history as the place through which all armies must pass that go North or South. At Stirling the train turned northeast and I noticed fields of brilliant yellow patchworking the green tableau from my window. These turned out to be [5]Rapeseed, grown for oil, a crop the government paid a subsidy for farmers to

4. For the purposes of easy narration, I shall refer to all fans of the Outlander series and books as 'Outlanders' from now on.
5. We know it as Canola Oil

grow. I was to see many of these bright yellow fields throughout my journey, and this late spring they were all nearing maturity.

The journey to Perth took an hour and a half, and at 11.40 I was dragging my bags out on the platform and heading to the bus station further down the road. Having an hour or so before the bus left, it was disappointing to find the only cafe servicing the bus terminal was closed, and only a small newsagent open. Nevertheless, I dragged all my bags in – effectively blocking the narrow aisles – while I bought something for lunch. When the bus for Crieff drew in to the bay, I was thrilled to see it was a double-decker, and lodging my bags downstairs in a cavity beside the driver, was soon upstairs and in the front seat with an amazing view of the road ahead. I watched Perth pass by with delight mingled with amazement, as the tall bus negotiated what felt like very narrow spaces and corners, almost brushing the brick walls of shop facings or scraping the sides of cars parked on the roadside. On this, my first experience (this trip) of being driven on Scottish roads I was impressed – again – with the dexterity with which large vehicles negotiated narrow lanes and the impossibility it seemed that so many cars could move through urban streets. I was watching closely, because on this trip I intended to rent a car and drive myself around Scotland, and I was beginning to feel a tad nervous. I made a mental note to avoid central Perth (ha!) and my fears only subsided slightly upon rolling out on to rural roads. Where were the passing bays, the sidings, the shoulders – all those useful areas of land on the side of a busy road into which you could pull over to check a map or let someone pass you? In fact, there were very few, but as it happened, by the time I eventually got behind a wheel, it didn't matter too much.

It was pleasant softly undulating country, with every now and then a small village to pass through, made up of tidy brick or stone homes and spring gardens. In New Zealand, many of our houses are made of wood, with tile or corrugated iron roofs, and so these sturdy buildings were delightfully different.

My bus – a Stagecoach number 15 – pulled in to High Street

in Crieff at 2pm, depositing me in the middle of a meandering street of old shops, some cobbles, a central seating area with the requisite memorial, and to my surprise, some sturdy slopes. When studying a map of Crieff from the comfort of one's studio in Auckland, I had neglected to take in topographical considerations. What looked like a level and easy walk to and from the Crieff Hydro Spa Hotel was in fact, various elevations of streets and some of those rather winding and narrow.

I soon found the Comely Bank Guest House on Burrell Street, happy to finally get my bags in the door. I paid £37 for a night here, sharing a bathroom with any other guests. The owner opened the door to me, with the words that check in was 4pm, and he was "just going out, so I was lucky to have caught him." I was only too happy to put cases down upstairs in my pretty little room and lie down for a bit. As it happened my host, Ron, wore various guises, only one of them being an owner of this B&B. He was also on the council, and was knowledgeable about Outlander being filmed at Drummond Castle just 3 miles outside town, as well as being a ticket dispenser and sales person at that same castle, which I discovered a few days later, when filming had finished. Seeing him there then, I had begun to think all Crieff men looked the same!

Leaving the house at 5pm I went in search of coffee, and found a nice little cafe serving Italian coffee in the area by the 'cenotaph'. I was wearing my [6]"Outrageous Outlander' t-shirt and had tidied up as best I could in preparation for meeting more Outlanders at the Hydro that evening. I was starting to feel a little nervous by now, and more than a little worried that after the confident brash persona captured in my memes, those who recognised me from those funny composites would find me a disappointment. Further up the narrow streets I went, following a GPS signal that – surprisingly – was working on my phone. I need not have worried; all uphill roads seem to end at the vast car park that surrounds the Hydro, and pressing on further up I found the main entrance and went in.

6. www.facebook.com/outrageousoutlander

The Hydro is a palatial arrangement of creamy buildings built with an Olde World charm and a hint toward the Grecian. Stately parks, clusters of tall trees, a hint here and there of outdoor activities like golf, all were impressions I got as I ducked between showers of rain into the main building. Some little hopeful part of me was vaguely expecting recognition straight away from various small clustered groups – I had been spoilt by Susan W in Edinburgh! It was not to be. And I gradually realised that the Hydro had much more on than

just our Outlander Gathering that weekend. Business men and women passed me in chatting groups heading to a meeting somewhere, families strolled in and out, pulling luggage and children along with them, one or two women dressed more casually, like me, glanced at me as they walked by. I smiled at them tremulously. Finally I sat down in the foyer and waited – hoping I would recognise someone, or they would recognise me. A woman I came to know, called Sheila, went past with her bags and came over to say hi! (She knew me, but I had yet to put faces to names.) Sheila said she would be down soon and went off in search of her room. I gave up sitting there and stood; contemplating walking back to my B&B and then it occurred to me that: 'what self-respecting Outlander fan would be sitting in the foyer when there was a bar nearby?' And so I followed all the signs for the bar, and sure enough, wide doors opened into a very busy, noisy room, filling quickly with what could only be vast hordes of Outlanders. To my great relief, a few called out to me from the corner and I advanced eagerly toward them, to find they knew me from my posts and memes. They were a mixed selection of friendly UK Outlanders, and two of the most vocal were from

Manchester and displaying the sort of wit I had grown accustomed to in a Mancunian friend of mine. In a few minutes I was nestled in a very comfy armchair, nursing a cocktail and burbling happily to these people I had never met before, and yet felt right at home with. I shall always be grateful for their friendliness particularly. Throughout the course of the next three days, [7]Jane and Sarah, particularly, included me in their activities, sat with me at mealtimes and generally kept me in a state of ebullient humour whenever I was with them.

After cocktails we all descended upon one of the in-house restaurants – a place with booths and round tables, and

there set to on some more substantial fare, laughing all the while and trying to hear each other over the racket. Various others came and went, introducing themselves and moving on to other tables, and all in all, it was a lively and ebullient start to the long weekend. By

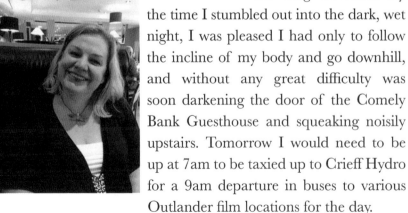

the time I stumbled out into the dark, wet night, I was pleased I had only to follow the incline of my body and go downhill, and without any great difficulty was soon darkening the door of the Comely Bank Guesthouse and squeaking noisily upstairs. Tomorrow I would need to be up at 7am to be taxied up to Crieff Hydro for a 9am departure in buses to various Outlander film locations for the day.

7. May or may not be their real names

Friday 15 May
Crieff

This day started with the usual overcast-but-not-raining weather, and I found the spacious 'cottage' dining room in which breakfast would be served downstairs. I had the choice of any of six gingham covered tables, and sat alone while Marion prepared my lavish breakfast, bedecked with a white chef's apron and cap. I had ordered a taxi in time to get me to the Crieff Hydro and the buses, and with great efficiency was deposited at the swinging doors of the hotel in good time.

There were two buses leaving for film locations from Crieff, another would leave from Glasgow and another from Edinburgh, and we were each circling the three locations on our itinerary so as not to put too great a strain on each place. I left my bags in the care of the reception staff, who said my room would be waiting for me upon return. Naturally, I found myself swept into the raucous company of the party from the previous night, and settled into the larger of the two buses. Our bus was bound for Castle Doune first, a mere 30 minutes away, and to pass the time I got out some copies of the theme song for the Outlander series I had printed off and passed them round. Some of us sang with greater gusto than others, but the song rippled around the bus:

Crieff
Comrie
Crieff
Perth
Muthill
Kinkell Bridge
Bridge of Earn
Dalchruin
Dunning
Greenloaning
Glendevon
Kinross
Milnathort
Doune Castle
Dunblane
Ben Cleuch
Yetts o' Muckhart
Wallace Monument
Castle Campbell
Bridge of Allan
Alva
Dollar
Tillicoultry
Tullibody
Alloa
Stirling
Clackmannan
Dunferm-line
Oakley
The Pineapple
Cowie
Airth
Kincardine
Culross
Grange-mouth
Bo'ness
Denny
Larbert
Falkirk
Hopetoun House
Polmont
Cumber-nauld
Slamannan
Linlithgow
Broxburn
Blackness Castle
Edinburgh

Sing me a song of a lass that is gone
Say, could that lass be I?
Merry of soul she sailed on a day
Over the sea to Skye

Billow and breeze, islands and seas
Mountains of rain and sun
All that was good, all that was fair
All that was me is gone

Sing me a song of a lass that is gone
Say, could that lass be I?
Merry of soul she sailed on a day
Over the sea to Skye *

Doune Castle is a popular castle for movies, and known by Outlanders as the seat of the McKenzies, or Castle Leoch, however it is also famous for 'Monty Python and the Holy Grail' and the 'Game of Thrones' to name a couple. We had blue skies when we entered through the gates into the courtyard and all that could be heard for a while was the soft 'shicking' sound of hand-held devices taking photos. As one who knows these places intimately, (because I've photo-shopped myself into many of the scenes,) it was easy to see where the filming had happened. This was my very first castle visit in Scotland, and so every worn circular stone stairway, every irregular arrow cleft, the arches and vaults and fireplaces so large you can stand in them, were thrilling. I took photos from every possible angle, and did not hesitate to climb to the very top, puffing and gripping the rope handrail firmly. Nor would it be the last time I wondered how a woman wearing a flowing bolstered dress with petticoats and bum roll could possibly have negotiated these narrow irregular stairways. Perhaps that relatively young median age at which a woman died back then was due to so many falls from castle steps, (and childbirth of course.)

*Words and music by Bear McCreary

✓ Bus tour

1

DOUNE CASTLE ✓

The stunning Doune Castle, near Stirling, plays a leading role in the show substituting for the fictional Castle Leoch – home to Colum MacKenzie and his clan in the 18th century episodes. It also features in the 20th century episode where Claire and Frank visit the castle in ruins on a day trip.

Once a royal residence, Doune Castle – although now in a ruined state – is still full of charm. Take a tour and find out how grand banquets would have once been prepared in the kitchen and servery as well as admiring its striking 100 ft high gatehouse and beautifully preserved great hall.

✓

12

Bus tour ✓

BLACKNESS CASTLE

Standing looking out over the Firth of Forth near Edinburgh is impressive Blackness Castle. This 15th century fortress provides the setting for the Fort William headquarters of Black Jack Randall as well as featuring in the heart-wrenching scene of Jamie's incarceration.

The castle was built by one of the most powerful families in Scotland, the Crichtons, and is often referred to as 'the ship that never sailed' due to its ship-like shape.

✓ Bus tour.

CULROSS

The rustic town of Culross in Fife is a unique example of what a town in Scotland would have looked like during the 17th and 18th centuries. It saw its Mercat area transformed into the fictional village of Cranesmuir – the home of Geillis Duncan and her husband Arthur. A stroll along the town's charming cobbled alleyways is about as close to stepping back in time to the 18th century as you can get.

Behind the impressive historic Culross Palace is where you can find the gorgeous herb that Claire works in in the grounds of the fictional Castle Leoch. It's planted with law and vegetables of the period – a real highlight for a true Outlander fan.

From the parapet, I could see more buses arriving, and so descended to the lawns, and from there to another filming location not so well known: the stream where Jamie bounces pebbles across the current, and is met by Leoghaire. Naturally, I had a go at tossing a flat rock or two, but sadly no red-headed kilted Scot emerged from the far shore. Jane had joined me for the wander to the river

and we both took photos. Bluebells were dotted throughout the grass and woodland, and it was all rather picturesque.

With just a minor delay – me – our bus departed for the next location; another castle, this one being Blackness Castle in Linlithgow, some

40 minutes away. It is indeed a much blacker place, used as a garrison, a prison, and munitions depot for much of its life. It also had a blacker background within the Outlander series, being Fort William where Jamie was whipped by Black Jack Randall. Talking of whipping, we took our packed lunches out to a wind-whipped table and ate them here, but the cutting breeze soon drove us into the fortress itself.

From Blackness castle to the final location, Culross village, is another 30 minutes. I think I enjoyed this location more than the other two combined. This picturesque village on the River Forth is made up medieval streets, ancient buildings and courtyards, and to top it off, a small but elegant Palace painted butter yellow, which dates from 1597. A busy 17th-century herb and vegetable garden fills the slopes behind the palace, where Claire and Geillis were

From the parapet, I could see more buses arriving, and so descended to the lawns, and from there to another filming location not so well known: the stream where Jamie bounces pebbles across the current, and is met by Leoghaire. Naturally, I had a go at tossing a flat rock or two, but sadly no red-headed kilted Scot emerged from the far shore. Jane had joined me for the wander to the river and we both took photos. Bluebells were dotted throughout the grass and woodland, and it was all rather picturesque.

With just a minor delay – me – our bus departed for the next location; another castle, this one being Blackness Castle in Linlithgow, some

40 minutes away. It is indeed a much blacker place, used as a garrison, a prison, and munitions depot for much of its life. It also had a blacker background within the Outlander series, being Fort William where Jamie was whipped by Black Jack Randall. Talking of whipping, we took our packed lunches out to a wind-whipped table and ate them here, but the cutting breeze soon drove us into the fortress itself.

From Blackness castle to the final location, Culross village, is another 30 minutes. I think I enjoyed this location more than the other two combined. This picturesque village on the River Forth is made up medieval streets, ancient buildings and courtyards, and to top it off, a small but elegant Palace painted butter yellow, which dates from 1597. A busy 17th-century herb and vegetable garden fills the slopes behind the palace, where Claire and Geillis were

filmed filling their baskets from the garden. Culross was the fictional village of Cranesmuir in the series, and it certainly felt as if we were strolling into the pages of a film set. We had a guided tour through the village and Palace, (stopping to have photos with our ears nailed to the pillary in the square), and finished up amongst the rows of herbs, hearing the herbalist who advises the show, Claire MacKay, give us her own description of herbal medicine and various plants in the gardens.

The bus arrived back at Crieff Hydro in the late afternoon, and I was given my door card and told to go to an outside building where my room was situated. It was raining so I ducked wetly into the foyer and searched for my room number. Bear in mind, I fully expected, having been a late registrant, to be sharing a room with four others – perhaps even a bunk! Imagine my amazement when the door I opened led into a spacious and luxurious bedroom, with wide views over the valley, deep armchairs, shower and bath,

and super king bed. Despite the fact that the key would not have opened the wrong room, I really did check the door number again. I had this room all to myself!? It was an unexpected, certainly undeserved, treat. To this day I do not know if I was upgraded, or if this was indeed the room I took over from the ones who had cancelled, but whatever the circumstances, I felt rather spoiled.

I lingered as long as I could luxuriating in all the splendor of my surroundings but then had to prepare for the dinner and 'Welcome' that would be happening in the special room we had for all our Outlander festivities. Gathering up all my courage, I dressed in my Outrageous Outlander costume, and slipped into the main building to find the signs that led to our venue. The lights were low, the round tables all had white linen cloths on them, candelabra sparkled from the centre of each, and I started looking for my name tag. My costume was a roaring success. Passing by various tables, more than a few called out my name or hailed me as 'sniskybobfry' or Jenny – which made me relax and start to feel very much at home. My own table was on the far side of the room, and we introduced ourselves and started getting to know one another. Despite wearing my costume and having a sturdy following on twitter and facebook, it still surprised me when occasionally someone tapped me on my shoulder to introduce herself and get a photo with me because she loved my memes. (To this day, I'm still surprised.)

After a buffet dinner, the evening entertainments began,

Above: Angela and I

which mainly centred around the giving of the Standing Stone Awards for everything from Best Body Part in a Scene to Wittiest Line heard. Having been a late entry to the UK Gathering, I am a little uncertain how those category winners were chosen and can only deduce they were selected through questionnaires online.

Let me take this moment to say that the whole event was well organized and appeared to run particularly smoothly. There were only minor hiccups in a weekend I would gladly attend again. The other thing I noticed were the large number of administrators who all appeared to share the burden of planning and executing this event, and a second tier of 'companions' to do more mundane tasks at the event. Naturally they were all thanked and so the evening wound to a close. I have a blurred memory of wandering among people, sitting at tables, getting lots of photos taken and taking some myself. Standing by the cardboard standee of Black Jack and kissing his cheek (this was before I had viewed episodes 15

and 16), and insinuating myself between the standees of Claire and Jamie. I was introduced to many people, and instantly forgot who they were when my back was turned, unless I could see their twitter name. Fortunately the long weekend afforded me a few times when I would see those same people again, and on my trip around Scotland I met a number of them once more. By THAT time, I had at least a handful of names well established in my memory bank. I apologize now to any I offended by my lack of recognition then and later. One of the photographers doing the rounds looked quite professional, and at one point introduced himself to me as coming from the Scottish Herald. He asked if he could photograph me, and we grabbed the life-sized cardboard Jamie, took him outside, and I gave him a peck on the cheek. It was all over in a few minutes, and I did not give it much more thought than that.

The day closed with me luxuriating in a deep bath, wishing I could stay awake to enjoy the amenities my own room provided, but I remember nothing once my head sank into the mountain of pillows.

Saturday 16 May
Crieff

There are some days when you wake up already sensing it is going to be a day packed full of great excitement, unexpected revelations, forever memorable moments. I had no idea upon waking that this was going to be 'one of those days'.

I read my programme this morning and saw that there was something called an 'Outlander Fayre' at 10am and so I got ready to go down for an early breakfast. This time I remembered to take a gift for Angela, one of the organizing team, from a fellow kiwi and friend, Rhonnie. At this point Angela told me that the Scottish Herald who had taken the photo on the previous night, wanted to interview me over the phone. We tried the number but it was busy, so made a plan to call later. Photo taken with Angela, I helped myself to the breakfast buffet, and then we all wandered down to see the various stalls and items being presented in the Melville Hall. The place was buzzing: there were stalls around the circumference selling everything from silver Celtic designed jewellery (I saw silversmiths from Edinburgh who had sold me my hipflask), genealogy maps, candle and soap makers, through to the bakers who supply the Outlander film crew. In the middle of the room were long tables on which – to my great delight – were some of the clever folk who work with Terry Dresbach on the costumes, and examples of their embroidery and clothing on display. A man was showing how to lay out a plaid and put it on, and to my further surprise, he turned out to be Ronnie B. Goodwin who has appeared in four episodes of the show. [8][Click]

I was handed Angela's phone at this point, and wandered outside to chat to the newspaper reporter and then handed the phone back, wondering if anything would come of it. By the time I found a long table set up with tartan cloth, and sat down to join the women 'waulking the wool' and singing rather wobbly Gaelic along

8. This parenthesis will denote photo opportunities taken.

with Ainsley Hamill, my happiness (I thought) was complete. On the stage near us Gillebride MacMillan, who had played the part of the bard in early episodes at Castle Leoch, was singing lilting Gaelic airs.

And then a distant rumble of mounting noise and excitement caught our attention and stopped the song. I began to hear the murmurs around me:

"The Outlander drivers are here – look!" followed closely by

"RON MOORE is here, that's him isn't it?"

"Oh my God! It's Terry too – she's come!"

I whipped around to look at the milling crowd by the door, and sure enough, clad in black leather jackets and hand in hand, Ron and Terry were smiling and moving toward the centre of the room. I must apologize right now to the table at which I was enjoying wool waulking, it reveals something of my lack of self-control and over-impetuousness that they were forgotten in a moment. I mumbled some excuse and clattered out of my chair, to join a growing group of fans keen to meet the beloved Producer and his Very Clever Wife. (If you read my Scottish bucket list points, you will see I only ever hoped for a glimpse of Terry from a distance). Heaven knows what Terry thought when she saw this tall purple apparition approaching through the haze of other faces, but she appeared to recognize me and smiled. It all happened very quickly and in somewhat of a blur. [Click] I can't [Click] even remember [Click] what I said, but the [Click] photos say it all. By the time I had met them both and had photos taken, and had a conversation with Ron about – of all things – the time it takes to fly from New Zealand to Scotland, (SIGH! Well, he asked!) they had moved on to other eager faces. Only then did I remember I had a calendar of my sketches in my bag, and hadn't got signatures or anything to write on for my other friends waiting at home. Nearby, and showing more acuity than I, Florida fansite administrator Tricia handed me a small poster and suggested I use that for signatures for Rhonnie.

I calmly awaited another opportunity to do just that and they were both gracious enough to meet me again and sign the poster for Rhonnie, [Click], and Terry received my calendar of Outlander sketches with what looked like genuine enthusiasm. [Click].

As if I was not already overwhelmed with the joy of meeting Ron and Terry, there was a further cluster of other Outlander 'celebrities' dotted around the hall. I met and briefly chatted with a friendly Ira Steven Behr, one of the writers, [Click], before moving over to have a chat with the Outlander drivers who I have tweeted regularly. [Click]. Somewhere I missed meeting another writer, Anne Kenney, who wrote my favourite episodes: 'The Wedding' and 'To Ransom a Man's Soul'.

When we went over to have lunch at the hotel restaurant, I was pleased to find that the 'celebs' were joining us. There I had a brief chat with Maril Davis [Click] and watched covertly as all of these fine folks ate and chatted in the middle tables of the room. If only I'd thought to get out my whisky flask and get the photo with the drivers at that point, I could have crossed off one of my bucket list points.

After lunch, without a break, we scurried down to a small conference room, where the afternoon session was shortened to give way to an impromptu Questions & Answers panel of Ron, Terry, Maril, Ira and Anne. There were no photographs allowed, nor recording of what was said, but I thoroughly enjoyed seeing them all together and watching a costume put on a slim lass on stage. Ira and Anne were verbose and lively speakers (surprise!) and had many anecdotes of how they had approached their work, and why they had chosen a particular angle to take on the episode they worked on.

It was a long afternoon with a full programme and by the end of it I was pretty tired after such full on sensory overload. Clutching all my purchases, bags, and papers to me, I made my way back to my room and collapsed for a few minutes on the bed, or so I thought. When I awoke, it was still — of course — very light

outside, and I glanced at my clock to see I was already late for dinner.

Without checking my programme, I pulled on a coat and shoes, and hurried through a near empty foyer down to the special hall we had set aside for Outlander events. Imagine my shock when I opened the double doors and walked into a dimly candlelit room, twinkling with soft light, and the candlelight twinkling on the jewels and baubles bedecking the formal attire of everyone seated at the round tables. I found my place and sat, needing no introduction but definitely underdressed for the occasion. It was a moment's decision to murmur my regrets and hasten back out of the room and up through the building, across the courtyard to my own room again. That was the fastest change into my costume and corset I have ever done, and with flushed cheeks and tripping over my long dress, I returned the same way to my place at the table. What a relief.

This was a formal dinner with the courses served at each table, and I had not missed anything as yet, except some opening words and banter.

The meal was in three courses and I remember thinking how well they had done for so large a company. I cannot tell you in any detail what I ate, but I can say I ate every crumb.

Following dinner, there was the usual moving about among tables and chatting, as the plates were cleared and furniture shifted to make way for the ceilidh. When I returned from a stint outside to cool my cheeks in the chilly garden, it was to find Skipinnish on stage and warming up. This is a band of five young men from the West Coast of Scotland, who play both traditional and modern instruments in their own style, championing 'classic Scottish Highland West Coast music'. I had already listened to various of their songs on iTunes after [9]Sam Heughan had put out some supportive tweets about them. Had he himself planned to surprise us, this would likely have been the moment. (Sadly, for me, he, Tobias and Cait were at this very moment attending Grant's

9. If you haven't guessed already, this is the actor who plays Jamie Fraser in the show Outlander

Edinburgh show).

It didn't take us long to warm up to the music and shortly after the dancing started in earnest, a group of Swedish Outlanders approached me and introduced themselves, saying they were fans of my memes. One of them asked to dance with me, and I was  very pleased to have such a keen partner for the lively dancing. Abandoning all hope of decorum, I twisted and wheeled around the floor, slipping regularly on my dress train, and feeling my corset sag downwards, under too much strain to be borne. I can only imagine how bouncy I must have looked to the observers on the sidelines. Well, actually, I was given photographic evidence later, for which I am mightily grateful. I was having a wonderful time, and fulfilling one of the bucket list points requiring dancing the night away. Had I any notion of how funny I must have looked, I might have been more subdued and conscious of my drooping costume, but it is probably just as well I didn't.

Toward the midnight hour, with the band slowing to a close, those of us remaining in the hall linked hands crossways and formed a huge circle, swaying to 'Olde Lang Syne' or something similar. After the previous two nights, although it was the only time I'd wear it, it had been worth filling a third of the lid of my case with the Outrageous Outlander outfit. From now on, it was just ballast.

Sunday 17 May
Crieff

I awakened on Sunday morning to yet another cool overcast day, but it was not raining and so the promised Highland Games would still be on. When I opened my door to go to breakfast, it was to see the Sunday Herald lying outside, and I remembered the interview and photo that had been taken of me. With nervous fingers I flicked through the pages looking for the article I expected to see of the Gathering with an assortment of our photos. Imagine my surprise upon seeing a large photo of my buxom figure leaning over to plant a kiss on cardboard Jamie's cheek at the top of page 16. Aside from a picture of Jamie and Claire on a horse, it was the ONLY photo supporting an article headlined: 'Fans from around the globe celebrate Outlander at Scottish gathering.' And within the page-long article were many quotes I had made about my trip from New Zealand and my experience so far in Scotland. How I can gush! Honestly, listen: "Jenny Jeffries, 59, from Auckland . . . top of her wishlist. . . dedicated fan. . .dresses in costume. . .Photoshops herself into scenes from the TV series. . .been overwhelming in a way. . . hooked on the series . . . blah blah blah". I hastily drew the significant section of the paper out and placed it on top of my bag to be packed later – all to no avail in the end, as the housekeeping staff are almost TOO efficient, and it was gone upon return.

With more bounce in my step, and my ego unneccssarily

Fans from around the globe celebrate Outlander at Scottish gathering

'OUTLANDER EFFECT' TAKES HOLD IN SCOTLAND AS DEVOTEES OF TIME-TRAVELLING ROMANCE DESCEND ON CRIEFF.
BY JUDITH DUFFY

Outlander fan Jenny Jeffries from New Zealand at the gathering   Photograph:

I T is a £50 million hit television show filmed in Scotland which has attracted a global fan following, and this weekend 200 enthusiasts from around the world have gathered in Perthshire to celebrate all things Outlander.

Devotees of the steamy time-travelling romance ventured to Crieff from as far afield as Australia and New Zealand with fans from US, Canada, France, Germany, Belgium, Spain, Sweden, Finland and Denmark also attending the get-together.

The sold out event – for which tickets cost around £200 – included visits to film location sites, costume displays and ceilidhs, and was organised by fan club Outlandish UK.

Jenny Jeffries, 59, from Auckland, New Zealand, said a trip to Scotland was top of her wish list this year – and when she heard the Outlander gathering was happening decided to make the long trip from Down Under.

The dedicated fan has a following of people on social media who enjoy her Outlander "meme" creations - where she dresses up in costume and Photoshops herself into scenes from the TV series with humourous captions.

She said: "Meeting other Outlander fans has been a dream come true. I have been very welcomed and made to feel part of the Outlander family – it feels like this is a lot of where the Outlander world is

"I was walking in Edinburgh to go to the railway station and a woman called out my name – and I realised she knew me from the Twitter and Facebook world.

"It has been overwhelming in a way, not only is it exciting seeing all these people, they also know me from my persona I put out there and it is exciting to get to know them."

Jeffries said she became hooked on the Outlander series of books after listening to an audiobook while travelling into work and has now read all of them twice. She is writing a blog about her trip to Scotland and plans to travel the country for another three weeks.

The Outlander series – based on the hugely popular books by US author Diana Gabaldon – is being filmed at studios in Cumbernauld as well as a series of locations around This includes Doune Castle, which per cent boost in visitors last year a the "Outlander effect".

Last year, tourism chiefs in Scotla a map of Outlander locations to ca the interest created by the show

The story follows married nurse dall, played by Caitriona Balfe, wh back in time from 1945 to the 18 through some mysterious standi where she finds adventure and ro chivalrous young Scottish warrior Ja played by Sam Heughan.

The Outlander gathering began to will end today with a Highland Ga money for charity and a screening episode of the TV show released Several names associated with the popped in yesterday, including ex ducer Ronald D Moore and costu Terry Dresbach.

Angela Sasso, one of the organise landish UK Gathering, said aroune were attending from 16 countries ble the number who had attended event last year.

She said: "Once you start to re you become quite passionate abou is something about these books people together and makes them other like-minded people.

"They are intelligently written, woven stories – they have got sex and adventure and history and e ven together. Once you become you want to meet other people wh much as you do.

"It's a great opportunity for pe gether and talk about the books ries has become a catalyst for get

Meeting other Outlander fans has been a dream come true. I have been very welcomed and made to feel pa the Outlander family – it feels like this is a lot of where Outlander world is. I was walking in Edinburgh to go railway station and a woman called out my name – an realised she knew me from the Twitter and Facebook

boosted, I made my way down to the buffet breakfast where I was regularly shown or made aware of the newspaper article by various Outlanders who had seen it. I'd like to say I received it all humbly, but I feel sure I was walking with an unbecoming swagger by the time we went up to the minibuses to go to the 'Games'.

These were held in a large field a small distance from the Hotel, and upon arriving en masse before a marquee, were addressed by a pleasing line up of nine kilt-clad athletes who were to be our 'trainers'. These able men separated us into eight teams and the competitions began.

Spread out around the field we were introduced to gumboot tossing, caber-throwing, haggis hurling, archery, relays with the haggis, and a tug-o'-war. All of my unbearable feelings from childhood athletic days threatened me, but I put on a bold show. Nothing much has changed both in outcome or performance since those days, but at least I was among friends performing similarly. All in all, I sweated off a bit of the substantial breakfast I had eaten, and lost some of the unpleasant swagger from my recent fame. The rain that threatened did not eventuate until the afternoon, and so we feasted for lunch upon a barbecue cooked up before us in the pavilion on the field. At this point various farewells were said, and addresses exchanged, and with sadness we watched a large portion of the attendees go back to the Hotel to pack and leave. I farewelled my own share of new friends, including the Manchester lasses. It would be a much reduced group who gathered for dinner and to watch the latest episode of Outlander in the evening – episode 15.

I had signed up for an afternoon trip to see the local whisky distillery – a perfect cure for the combined effects of inflated ego and loss of new friends – and a handful of us squeezed into a taxi to go to the 'Famous Grouse' Distillery. Others had walked through scattered showers and were there before us. It is actually the Glenturret Distillery, (the oldest Distillery tour in Scotland), and

I enjoyed my first foray around the gleaming golden vats amidst the smell of barley being refined into something liquid and able to set your mouth on fire. Of course, I bought a small bottle and proceeded to fill my new 'Je Suis Prest' hip flask with it upon arrival back in my room.

At a little after 6pm, I set off for the 'Ferntower Suite' where a buffet dinner would be served after which we would watch Outlander. Arriving (again) a little late, I found all the comfy seating claimed and scattered hard chairs at the very back the only seats available. I didn't mind – knowing what the episode we were to see contained, I was loath to be seen sobbing like a girl up in the front rows, and knew I could snuffle quietly into my tissues unseen in the back. I reacquainted myself with a fan called Lynn, and we chatted until the show started.

It was a tough watch. There was nothing but silence and the movement of hands to eyes in the latter parts of the show. If we thought we had seen the breadth of Sam, Cait and Tobias' acting in the earlier parts of the series, we were wrong. There was much more they were capable of, and they delivered. And I had to leave the story hanging right there, with Jamie in the hands of Black Jack Randall, for another five weeks until I was home in New Zealand. It was going to be a strain but I knew the outcome from the books, and tucked it all away until later.

That last night it was a sober group of Outlanders who made their various ways off to bed.

I sank for the last time into the luxurious folds of linen encompassing me on the super king bed, reflecting on a day that had started with elation and ended with contemplation of what one human who has lost his soul can do to another. The weekend had promised to deliver rich experiences and had certainly done that.

Monday 18 May
Crieff

In no great hurry the next morning, I welcomed the chance to quietly pack and enjoy my immediate surroundings. By mid-morning the main foyer was filled with small groups occupied with hasty farewells and final words and I joined them before taking a taxi down to my next B&B: Galvelbeg House, on the main road through Crieff heading to Perth. This was a £45 night and positioned better for an easy walk to the bus stop the next day.

The gregarious owner was surprised to see me so early, but let me put my bags upstairs and I left to go and find a coffee and something to eat. I was beset with some complex feelings: about to start a month of driving myself around Scotland, alone, having just left a richly varied, fun-filled, social weekend at the Hydro. To be honest, I really didn't know how well I would do the 'traveling alone' thing, let alone the driving in a strange country. Before I had left New Zealand, occasional visions of black ice on the road in the Outer Hebrides and my car slipping unseen down a snowy slope and not found for weeks, had kept me awake. In the cold light of day it was easy to pooh pooh such fantasies, and now I was here I could see that the roads would hardly have ice on them, but still. I was missing [10]'my people'.

The cure for the state I found myself in was easy and obvious: keep moving. I walked into the centre of town and down to the café that offered Italian coffee – and the inevitable bakery item I found irresistible while I was over in the UK. Call it comfort food, call it researching local fare, or call it what it was: a carb addiction, it all tasted pretty good. From the café it was a short few doors downhill to a Cab Company sign, and so I opened the door and strode in. The person hunched behind the dim counter was on the phone and looked surprised to see me. He finished the call hastily and asked

10. This might refer to family and friends I often met with at home, or even the new ones I'd 'hung out with' at the Gathering: my kind of folk.

if he could help me, and at that point I understood that the usual method was to call the Cab company. Indeed, this did resemble the rather grotty interior to the Coronation Street business run by Steve McDonald and Lloyd Mullaney.

In some eagerness to get me out of the office, the owner indicated a car park over the road, and we hastened to it. The drive to Drummond Castle and gardens was not long, but I did not want to walk it, and was pleased I hadn't when we drove up the long stately drive between lush green trees. It was a precursor to even more splendour ahead. Dropping me at the entry gates, the taxi driver left me his card and drove off.

At the guardhouse, which proved to be the ticket office and shop, I encountered a familiar face: that of Ron, my B&B host of Thursday night. He was wearing one of his other hats, and we chatted for a short time about the filming of Outlander that had just occurred there in the previous week. It was not the last time I was to feel the 'so near and yet so far' sensation assail me. Indeed, taking the direction he had pointed me in, I could see over a wall into what had been the tented area where the crew had set up – a village? A market? Only time will tell. There were still hired outside lights awaiting pick up.

Drummond Castle is not open to the public, but it does not matter a jot, for the gardens most certainly are. When I approached the wall and stairs leading down into the spectacular geometrical arrangements of flora and statues below, I had to stop to catch my breath. A tiered arrangement of stairs and walls lead gradually down to a wide expanse of tightly maintained textures and colours in flower beds and hedges. It was a huge Persian tapestry of plants, flowers, topiary hedges, fountains, spreading like a carpet as far to the left and right as the eye could see until taller hedges blocked the view. The forward view stopped at a line of trees and a distant wood rose over the skyline, bisected by a broad walk.

Still staring in awe at the view below, I was surprised when

two women approached me from the top terrace and announced they were Outlanders and had recognised me. We chatted about the filming that had taken place here, and our future plans for traveling Scotland, before they headed off to walk the gardens. I was not alone after all. I ambled happily around the patterned pathways, taking photos and just enjoying the peace and tranquillity these gardens exude. The sun was positively beaming down, and when I found a bench to sit and eat my purchased lunch, it was almost too hot. I stayed for a long time pondering what to do next, now that I had no written schedule to follow.

Two hours later the taxi picked me up and took me back to town. I cruised the streets for a little while, popping into shops and making small purchases, including a set of studs for my ears set with dark blue stones, which I wore for the duration of my trip. I found a small museum in the information centre under the clock tower, and paid to go down and peruse it. It was not very big but it certainly made an impact on me when I looked into the room marked The Crieff Stocks and saw a very Jamie-looking model with his feet in the stocks. Considering the image of Jamie we had been left with after the last episode viewed the previous night, it was a sad reminder of his fate. I left this handsome red-headed fictional fellow to his own fate as well, and went up to the sunlight again.

Time for a break from sensory overload back in my room at the B&B. My room had two single beds in it and an ensuite, and was perfectly comfy, although it overlooked the main road and was therefore quite busy. A group of four male Swedes had parked their motorcycles behind the house and could be heard clattering up the stairs and talking. Dinner was a short walk away at a restaurant called The Tower, and I was pleased to be offered a table in the alcove window with views out across the valley. It was a tasty meal of slow-braised beef on mashed potato with baby vegetables, which I ate dreamily gazing out at the view. I followed it with Pistachio and Raspberry Mess, a dessert I would love to see take hold back home.

After dinner I settled into my room and started going through my plans for the coming day: when the bus would leave for Perth, where to pick up the car etc. I had already written the details into a small school notebook I took with me everywhere, but I just wanted to check the Google map overview of the streets I'd need to navigate. It didn't seem long before I descended into sleep, waking at 4am with the sun and wondering if I'd ever get used to the short nights.

Tuesday 19 May

Crieff to Fife

At 7.30 I was downstairs, the first guest to await my bacon, eggs, sausage and toast in another pleasant table by the window. The Swedish bikers arrived soon after and with squeaking leather pulled out chairs and awaited their own meals, talking volubly in a language I didn't know.

The bus stop was just across the street and my B&B host helped me drag my bags out of the house to the kerb. At precisely 9.10 another double-decker bus drew up and I relinquished my luggage to the baggage racks, ascending to the top deck once more. It was a completely different sensation to be driven away from a spectacular weekend and into a future in which you yourself will be behind the wheel. One thing I was looking forward to was having a permanent space into which I could put my bags and sundry other bits and pieces. A small moving room on wheels all to myself. . . a place I might even sleep in, if I could not find a vacancy.

The bus retraced the same route back in to Perth and drew in to the station at 9.48. I disembarked and began the process of pulling two wheelie bags along a pavement slightly too narrow for them. Every now and then I would check my I-phone to see where the GPS was leading me too. It didn't look far, but the signal was unstable and the software thought I was a car. On and on I walked, dodging awkwardly across busy streets, rattling over a bridge, wheeling noisily down a suburban road. . . wishing, after all, I had caught a taxi. I finally pulled in to the unassuming carpark outside Europcar on Glasgow Road, and then opened the office door and dragged everything in there. So relieved was I to be there at last I gushed enthusiastically over the counter only tapering to a halt when I realised no one was listening. The young male I had been talking to was on the phone, but he disinterestedly reached a hand

up for my papers. My smile faded, but I hadn't given up yet. When his phone call was completed he started typing in details from my confirmation printout and then, dull-voiced, asked for passport and drivers license. I chattered happily as I handed them over, hoping for some repartee and feeling a bit nervous. Nothing. He did show some animation in offering me insurance for a sizeable increase in my total, and I declined. (Only later I remembered that my driving was covered under my travel insurance anyway.)

Then Mr Chatty pulled himself out of his seat and assessed the yard. I looked as well, liking the cars in the direction his head was turned. Without a word he moved out to that corner and disappeared from view towards a rather nice mid-sized row of cars. Then I saw him driving what turned out to be a small black VW Polo that had been hidden in the corner. This car reappeared at the entrance and drove up to the office. My helpful and chatty (NOT) young man got out and handed me the keys. I called him back to ask him a question about petrol cap opening and he mumbled, "Just push it." Sensing I 'was pushing it' myself, I got all my bags in without aid, turned the car on, and glancing nervously at the gears hoped my ability to drive manual had not faded. It hadn't. The car eased out on to one of the busiest roads in Perth and I had no time to think – my I-phone was not attached yet, I had no idea where I was going, and there were no places to pull over and sort that out. That first 30 minutes were among the most terrifying in my driving experience in Scotland: I drove up and down side streets unable to pull over with traffic breathing

heavily down my bumper behind me. Finally I found a car parking building and pulled in to double park and turn off the engine. I found my phone-holder, set up my I-phone with Google maps on it, set it for Falkland, one of the film locations we had not seen yet, and took a bracing breath. With great relief my friendly English-accented GPS guide told me exactly where to go, and I drove out more confidently, feeling my heart pulse less frantically as I left Perth in my rear-vision mirror.

Falkland is 27 kms southeast of Perth and much sooner than I expected I found the car nosing its way into a perfectly delightful cobble-street town straight out of the film set. I was literally pulling up to the same kerb that Frank and Claire had pulled up to in the 1940's 'Inverness' that was the opening scene in Outlander. As one who has viewed that portion of footage numerous times, both on TV and plucking screen captures for my memes, I knew it intimately and was utterly entranced. I drove past the four-sided monument against which the ghost of Jamie had leaned, and turned left to find the car park. That done, I tripped down a cobbled walkway or two to arrive back at the centre of town, where I started taking photos. I literally followed Claire and Frank in my mind as I approached the very doorway they had walked to – Mrs Baird's guesthouse – and, not knocking, I walked in to what was in fact, a café and B&B. Passing the window on my way in, I noticed Jamie looking back out – Pocket Jamie of course. I believed I babbled incoherently for a while as the smiling hostess waited patiently, and something of my enthusiasm must have rubbed off, for she took me upstairs to view the very room from which Claire had brushed her hair as ghost Jamie watched. It was a bathroom, and rather difficult to reach the window, so the interior must have been done at the studio. Still, I felt I was definitely 'following Claire' and happily made my way downstairs for a light and very welcome refreshment in the bar area, gazing out on the square.

After that restorative break, I set off around Falkland

FALKLAND

5

ou can recreate one of the first scenes of the
V series in the town of Falkland in Fife,
hich substituts for 1940s Inverness.

ee if you can recognise the familiar cosy look
f *Mrs. Baird's Guesthouse* in The Covenant-
· Hotel – your heart is guaranteed to start
cing with excitement the instant you see it,
d you can stand by the Bruce Fountain
here Frank witnesses the ghost of Jamie
oking up at Claire in the first episode.
mpbell's *Coffee Shop* is just across the road
further down the street is Fayre Earth Gift
op which stood in for *Farrell's Hardware*
d Furniture Store where Claire stops to
k at the window stocked with authentic
iod merchandise.

village, looking for the window that held the vase Claire had gazed longingly at. I'm not sure I found it, but I did a bit of my own gazing longingly, and found a small gift shop where I purchased a cloth book with very pertinent quote: "Life begins at the end of your comfort zone" – Neale Donald Walsch.

On my way through the village I passed two more shop windows with Pocket Jamie looking benignly back at me, and smiled. I am sure I was not the first Outlander to pass by on the street. Ever fearful of running out of fruit or water, I purchased these at a small store, and then – reluctantly – left town, continuing on the southern route toward my next destination: Aberdour Castle, Fife.

This 12th century castle doubled as the monastery in France that Jamie flees to (last episode]. Up and down I spiralled, enjoying the polished wooden floors, painted ceiling, and sense of refined living it enjoyed as a 'luxurious Renaissance home'. The tiered lawns and pretty orchard were small but rather gorgeous, especially with spring blossoms on the boughs. But the pigeon house in the shape of a beehive was the most unusual feature – here the early owners kept pigeons for eating in the feasts held in the castle. Filming had mostly taken place in the ground floor entry and stabling area, but not a sign of recent occupation was present. I had a chat with the information centre attendant, and a hearty soup in the kitchen that had been converted into a café.

The Aberdour township surrounds the castle, winding old streets and a downhill slope to the broad River Forth. I was hopeful of staying in one of the characterful houses in this older part of town, and had marked a potential one right on the water. Driving down a narrower and windier road, which became so twisted and unused looking, that I turned back once and was forced to return, I rounded a steep corner and found that indeed, my cart-track WAS a road leading to a few old buildings ahead. There at the end was a dilapidated two-storey guesthouse, with no sign of occupants. I parked and knocked but received no response, nor was there an

ABERDOUR CASTLE

The delightful 12th century Aberdour Castle doubles as Sainte Anne de Beaupré's monastery in France which Jamie flees to; the castle's Old Kitchen and Long Gallery were used for filming.

Situated on the Fife coast, this splendid ruined castle was once a luxurious Renaissance home, and is amongst the oldest standing masonry castles in Scotland.

answer to my phone call. In the end I reversed and drove back up the way I had come, disappointed to find such a unique old hostelry right on the water was shut. As it was getting quite late in the day, I pulled in to the main street and enquired of the two hotels there, but at this early stage in my journey, their prices exceeded what I was willing to pay. Before panic set in, I managed to get a positive response on the phone to an inquiry about a B&B in Burntisland, Fife, (not far away), and so booked it then and there.

The place was called 'Martin's Lodge', which sounded rustic and I put in the address on my phone and followed instructions, only to be guided to a unassuming and rather ordinary two-storey house on a busy transit route in the new part of town. I parked and a perky woman with blonded hair and dressed in sparkly garments showed me upstairs to a large room with three beds crammed in it: a queen-size, and two singles. "I'll let you have the queen, as a special treat!" There was a pokey ensuite, and an area hidden behind the roofline and the wardrobe you could try and make a cup of tea in. Oh, and a balcony, "This room has a lovely balcony which is a feature" – that looked out on the backs of other suburban homes and enjoyed a slicing breeze in the spring evening. I did not avail myself of the view. It cost £50 for the night and the sturdy Scottish breakfast the next morning. I never met Martin after whom the Lodge was named, but I did enjoy my hostess's fondness for spangles, glittery objects, chandeliers and mirror tiles. I imagine he must too.

My evening meal was partaken in a pub that backed on to the river, in what I would get accustomed to enjoying in the UK: a family style eating and drinking establishment. In my homeland, pubs are generally rowdy drinking establishments, and not regarded as somewhere you would take your family for dinner. This one also had wifi, and so I settled into a comfortable booth and updated my blog.

Wednesday 20 May
Fife to Falkirk

Approaching my black car this morning to load my bags, I was dismayed to find it absolutely covered in bird droppings. My hostess brought out some spray cleaner and rag, and I did what I could to remove the evidence of seagulls in the area.

It was a beautiful blue morning, with a light breeze, and I stopped for photos of the Rapeseed fields bursting with brilliant yellow, along with yellow gorse, against a backdrop of the distant red Forth bridge. All was right with the world!

Today I turned southwest and crossed the bridge toward Edinburgh and into Linlithgow, birthplace of Mary, Queen of Scots. I parked and walked up the cobbled drive from the heart of town, to the Palace, passing signs indicating the Scottish rulers in chronological order along the way. Through the brick arch and into the courtyard, it is hard not to be impressed by the size of the palace

and the church on the right next door. To the left of the entrance area, there is an information centre and shop where you purchase your ticket. It costs about £8, but it was worth it. I also convinced the somewhat dubious kilted red-headed Scot who sold me a ticket, to pose for a photo in keeping with my Scottish bucket list points. Part of my purchases also included a beguiling little floral coronet, which seemed appropriate given it was a famous queen's palace. In honour of Mary, who I doubt would have been so frivolous, I wore the coronet as long as it took to take photos and from then on it graced the back window space of my car.

This former Stuart residence was ravaged by fire in the 18th century, but the core of the building remains, and I was able to climb stairways up three levels. The palace looks out upon verdant pastures and the Linlithgow loch. Inside, many of the rooms remain intact, and there is a strong sense of its original grandeur. Linlithgow Palace was also another of the filming locations for Outlander – not one I had yet seen – being the prison entrance and corridors used when Jamie was imprisoned.

During visits from 'Bonnie Prince Charlie', the ornate fountain in the main courtyard was said to have flowed with wine. It did not today. Feeling in need of refreshment, I walked back down to the main street and saw a quaint little coffee shop (another habit I couldn't shake), and so I entered to purchase coffee and whatever of the many pastries took my fancy.

Onward and upward! I planned to cover some ground today, and it was already lunchtime.

The next stop was nearby, in West Lothian, and only 9 minutes drive away, or about 5 kilometres. Bo'ness & Kinneil Railway doubled as the London railway station at which Claire and Frank bid farewell during the war. I wanted to go partly because of the film location, but also because my father, who had died three years ago, was a keen steam train fanatic, and I couldn't bypass the opportunity to see it.

It was a beautiful fresh spring day, but the station and all its surrounding engines, carriages, bridges and various mechanical ruins, were devoid of life. My car was the only one in the car park. I walked to the derelict station that would have been used for the filming, but encountered a major obstacle: a sign on the door said 'Closed' and the gate leading in was firmly bolted. From my position I was able to snap off a few shots with my zoom lens and was turning to go, when I noticed a young man shovelling coal off rail tracks some distance away. I called out to him, asking when the station would be open. I think he must have been desperate for a break from shovelling for he stopped, said he would find out if he could show me around, and disappeared off to talk to his superior. I was not sure what he was going to show me around – hopefully the station – I had told him I was an Outlander fan. I was about to learn afresh how very focussed and passionate steam engine aficionados really are.

His name was Owen, and he bounded over the tracks to open the gate onto the rails, not the station. In a few minutes I was picking my way carefully between greasy rolls of rope and equipment, into a huge shed full of engines. Owen introduced me to a shorter, older man, also wearing grubby blue overalls, who was tinkering at the working parts of a large green boiler. By mutual consent, no one shook hands – just brushing past them I acquired a small dark mark on my coat. It was actually rather fascinating being up close to so many steam engines. On the ground at the entrance lay some 'Thomas the Tank Engine' faces, recently removed from the engines after a family fun day. I can remember no specific facts from all that was told me, except a growing realisation that they had mistaken my own interest to be one for steam trains, and there was no connection to the Outlander filming in their heads at all. I didn't mind. I knew one or two enthusiasts back home who would have easily spent the day in the shed here and been in seventh heaven. For their sake I absorbed as much as I could. After showing suitable awe at the size and history of the engines in this shed, Owen led me through the extensive rail system filled with even more, to reach a back entrance into the actual museum. The tour did not stop there either. We picked up a man and his young son and continued all the way down through the building, arriving finally at the engine most recently being acquired and regarded as the jewel in the steam train museum 'crown'.

'Maude' is an immense black locomotive, weighing an impressive 126 tons, and built in 1935. She was taken to Turkey during the Second World War, and was used extensively until 1986. She will be the next big restoration project.

I was very ready to move on after seeing Maude. Leaving Owen still chatting to the man and his son, I thanked him and set off over the railway bridge and back to my car.

I wanted to finish this day with a delivery of a package to the Outlander studio in Cumbernauld, the signed-by-Kiwi-fans card, and gift of two greenstone pendants for Sam and Cait. In order to do that, I had planned a night in Falkirk, not too far from Cumbernauld (at which I had failed to find any accommodation). I booked this night at a hotel called The Antonine, which was right in the heart of town, and cost around £40, which suited me. How bad could it be? As it happened: Quite.

Following my GPS instructions, I eventually found The Antonine after negotiating a couple of one-way roads and going under a barrier arm. The front façade of the 'hotel' is dirty, dated and depressing. In fact there are a lot of 'd' words associated with this place: dingy, demoralising, dump come to mind as well. I dragged my bags in to the empty space in front of an un-manned counter, and soon a person strolled over from the door into the bar. He took my details and offered me a key, and indicated that I was on the second floor. I had to lift my cases up the first flight of stairs into what I hoped was a lift lobby. It was not. I lifted them up the next major flight of stairs and along a weird, deserted (another 'd' word) corridor in which lights flickered on as you walked past them; it felt like part of a horror film. At the end and through more doors, was a small ancient lift. I took it with some misgivings. My own room was a short walk from the lift doors upstairs, and was an equally dull space, with room for a bed, a bathroom, and windows looking out on other roofs and parking spaces. I stowed my few items, and refreshed myself, comforting myself with the knowledge it was only for one night. Back outside, I waited for the barrier arm to raise, and then drove to Cumbernauld and what I hoped was a successful delivery of our New Zealand card. At the last roundabout, with the huge warehouse in sight, I was distracted by shouts from some women in another car in the process of driving away. It was the couple of American fans whom I had met at Drummond Castle gardens, Crieff!

They pulled up beside me outside the main gates of the Outlander studios, and we wound windows down to talk. They had been there already hoping to find a way in to reception, and were staying at the nearby golf hotel. To be honest, I wanted the best chance of being able to deliver the gifts I had from New Zealand, and I doubted my chances would improve if there was a group of us, so I told them I would come and meet them at their hotel shortly. They told me that Sam and Cait were not at the studios, which they had discovered through some source, but I wanted to leave a note anyway, and after this exchange, they drove off.

I was a jumble of nerves throughout this whole studio visit. The unlikelihood of even seeing a passing car with any Outlander star in it was known, but I had come such a long way to stand now in the same street as the studio and was about to pass over the items that had been in my bag all this way. I was loath to pass on details of any of this visit on social media, because I knew the hardworking staff of Outlander discouraged taking photos of the studios. I feel that same constraint in telling this story, and so I won't detail it beyond saying that when I did get to speak to someone, I only handed over a map of where the card had gone, and a note along with one of my Outrageous Outlander photobooks. I wanted a second chance later on, at maybe meeting Sam personally to hand the card over.

The golf hotel was only a few blocks away, and Sharon and Julie (yes, I learned their names) were waiting in the bar. We had a drink and then went upstairs for dinner and exchanged stories of our travels so far. They were heading home to the Ohio in a couple of days. It was a comforting way to end a nerve-wracking experience, and I enjoyed some fellowship with other Outlanders, knowing I was off on my own again soon.

I left this luxury hotel for my substandard model after dinner, and followed my 'horror film' route back to the bleak bedroom to pore over maps and see what to do the following day.

Thursday 21 May

Falkirk to Tummel Bridge

The Antonine was below par for accommodation on my trip, but at least I left in the morning after a good night's sleep in a clean bed and having had a relaxing bath.

I set my GPS guide for Stirling castle, and hoped I'd end up at the Trossachs for the night via Callander, Balquidder and Tummel Bridge.

From Falkirk to Stirling it was an easy half an hour drive for 22 kms. On the way, however, I passed a signpost that said, 'Hopetoun House' and a bell went off in my head. I knew that Midhope Castle is on Hopetoun Estate and is the building that was used as Lallybroch in the show. Naturally I diverted from my chosen route in order to stop at [11]Lallybroch.

It was to be a much more complicated diversion than expected. I misinterpreted my instructions and did a bit of doubling back to get to the broad road with gatehouse that led to Hopetoun House. It is also a strange contradiction that the palatial residence passing as the 'House' is much more of a castle than the tall manor house called 'Midhope Castle'. But I diverge from my story again.

Upon parking, I approached the information centre only to be suddenly hailed on my way by a beaming auburn-haired Outlander, standing with a group of others, who recognised me from my memes. She regaled me with her own experiences of going to Lallybroch, telling me that she was with a tour group and probably that was the only reason they had been able to get on the estate. I approached the information officer with more trepidation, but need not have worried. She was very informative, and told me to apply to the Estate office for permission. They were in a building behind the trees, and informed me I would need to get a permit

11. Lallybroch is the family home for James Fraser

83

from the Hopetoun Farm Shop, which I remember passing some time earlier on my way here.

Back out to the main road I went, retracing my earlier drive here, and after a few miles found the Farm Shop. Once there it was a simple matter of handing over a few pounds, and signing an agreement not to disturb or disrupt any of the farm buildings etc. I took my permit, which was never sighted after that, and began the drive to 'Lallybroch'. The long way around as it happened. When I finally rounded the familiar bend and saw before me the long drive and very familiar building we have come to know as Jamie's home, my joy knew no bounds. The delight at arriving was worth all the effort to get there. I took photos, and drove up to the arched gateway, despite dogs barking wildly in the house next door.

I looked closely at the arch where Jamie had been whipped, and could picture Black Jack Randall standing there mopping his brow. [Shudder]

Now it was time to resume my journey to Stirling.

It would be hard to miss Stirling castle. For one thing, it is on a very high and obvious promontory. For another, all roads up to the Highlands seem to go past it (unless you take the Forth Bridge directly north from Edinburgh). And for another, so much of Scottish history features the castle, which was a 'favoured residence for Scotland's Kings and Queens', and it has recently undergone a huge makeover called 'the Palace Project'. It seemed obligatory for me to investigate how the years of research and construction have reformed the area known as the palace, home of Mary Queen of Scots, (as well as to actually see the costumed performers in action). I was not disappointed.

I parked down in the township and walked the steep cobbled hill up past the Duke of Argyll's old stately home, to cross the car park into the gatehouse area of the castle. (Anything to avoid yet more parking fees!)

The first impression I got was, 'wow, this place is huge!'

Left: Maryanne Meister and I at Hopetoun House (below)

Midhope Castle

There are many, many, crumbling ruins of castles dotted around Scotland – this is not one of them. Within the castle there is a lot of restoration happening – walls that are made of the same stone as the old castle, but quite golden in colour in their new state. I made my way through corridors with rooms leading off to interactive displays for children to participate in, other rooms with passive displays, all of them teeming with people. The newly restored palace area was the most interesting, because the tapestries were exceptionally good, and the furnishings of earlier periods need not be imagined – they were there, being used, by people dressed in period costume! The ceilings and walls were painted as they would have been originally and were exquisitely lavish in colour and detail. For the first time I wish I had been wearing my Outrageous Outlander costume for the palace tour, and had photos taken in situ. But nothing could beat the amazing view as I stepped out of the dimmer internal spaces onto the ramparts. This promontory is why Stirling castle was built here. What a commanding view in 360 degrees!

After soaking up the views, the internal halls and courtyards, and the stories that abound throughout the tour of the castle, I reached my saturation point and headed back down the hill to my car. It was time to get on the move again.

I set my GPS direction for Callander, a small town on the A84 from Stirling, and only about 20 minutes drive northwest. I had chosen Callander as a stopping point because it was historically the meeting point between the Highlands and the Lowlands. It would also lead me through Loch Lomond area and the Trossachs, where another portion of Outlander had been filmed.

Sure enough, despite the growing greyness of the day, the pretty little town emerged in front of my windscreen, a main street chock full of diversity and some beguiling businesses – many bakeries – and a museum or two featuring Rob Roy. Things were looking brighter indeed. I found parking around the back – pay and display of course – and took in the portion of extensive cycle path that crossed at this point. If I had been staying a day or so, I would definitely have hired a bike to investigate further.

Being lunchtime, the cafes and bakeries were humming, and I could not find a table at the two I tried. Instead I purchased the Scottish equivalent of a Cornish pasty – a bridie – and took it and a take away coffee back to the park by my car. While I munched very happily on my pastry, and discovered afresh that I had no signal on my phone, I flicked open the pages to the Lonely Planet Scotland that would be my mainstay throughout the trip. I called and booked a place near Kinloch Rannoch for the night that would cost £40.

Driving north out of Callander I glanced to my right and swerved the car to a halt. On the other side of the road, penned so that tourists could have a closer look, was a Highland 'Coo' munching on some hay. This was my first close up of one of these amazing animals since my last trip, and I welcomed the chance to get up close and personal with the shaggy face and lethal horns again. Despite the size and danger it is hard to feel anything but cuddly about them.

I saw my first decent-sized loch in the Highlands along this road: Loch Lubnaig. A white swan, sensing the important occasion, glided past just for my camera.

About 30 minutes drive north of Callander signposts appear pointing left down a narrow country road to 'Rob Roy's Grave' at Balquhidder. If, like me, you have been brought up on a diet of romance, adventure, and period drama, this Scottish hero's grave from the 1700s will be a must-see. My most recent memory of the story was the 1995 movie with Liam Neeson in the title role. That particular story had much fiction woven into it, so much so that I was almost surprised to find out he had actually lived and had a grave that could be visited. His story covers loss and evictions, the early Stuart rising, Jacobites and misdealings by the English, imprisonments, but remarkably, Rob lived until he was 80!

So begins my introduction to the first of many single-lane

winding roads over which I must learn to navigate. The road to Balquhidder astonished me because I thought it a private driveway, not a main thoroughfare for a town. It was to become something I took as commonplace almost from this point on.

There were only a few others picking their way slowly over the deserted ruins of a churchyard when I parked beside their cars and made my way up to look. It was actually quite moving to see the family plot, marked with its rousing 'MacGregor Despite Them' gravestone. (Some little Scottish part in me rose up and punched an arm in the air). Rob's is the middle grave, and on either side of him are his wife, (Helen) Mary and his son, Coll. A lone black sheep contemplated me, as I contemplated the graves, and we had a moment of peaceful reflection together.

Back on the main road (A84) again, I continued north through increasingly mountainous countryside.

Although it was spring, evidenced by bluebells occasionally dotting the fresh green foliage, the air was breezy and fresh and the sky threatening rain. The foothills of these rounded peaks were a patchwork of pinky-brown, yellow and green – up close this translated to heather, gorse or dried grass and new spring growth. Higher up, the rocky peaks were blunted and granite grey in appearance, with stubby green bushes dotting them (the biggest peaks were yet to be seen in this early part of my trip). I was still wearing my puffer jacket and a silly smile. Whenever a little township nestled against a picturesque river appeared, I would stop, stretch my legs, take a breather and a photo. These towns were uniformly filled with modest white houses which had slate or grey tile roofs and often a pretty stone bridge arched across the water.

By the time I had passed through Lochearnhead and reached the T-junction that leads west to Loch Lomond or east to Pitlochry, the sky was oppressively grey. I turned east. I remember driving this road with Loch Tay on the right glistening like molten silver, the leafy branches swaying gently overhead, and feeling like I was in a twilight world. It was afternoon, but there were no shadows of the boughs overhead on the road, and everything had taken on a dream-like quality. We rarely experience this kind of muted light in New Zealand, where the mid-day sun creates great contrasts of shadow or glaring brilliance under forest canopies.

In that same dreamy state, I turned off the road at the head of the loch, and went up a steep one-lane road heading directly north to Tummel Bridge. I had barely rounded two corners and gone past a passing bay, when I saw a huge fully laden logging truck bearing down on me, and another just behind it! Panic-struck I jammed on my brakes, found reverse, and backed down the hill swerving into the passing bay. With pounding heart I watched the trucks, which had hardly slowed, roar past in a cloud of dust, two grinning young men in the cabs of both. It took me a few minutes to collect myself, and find the courage to continue on that road – much slower and with greater caution than before. You have no idea the relief when I reached Tummel Bridge.

In fact, I did not go through Tummel Bridge, but turned west at the T-junction and headed towards Kinloch Rannoch. My accommodation for the night was to be at 'The Gardens Dunalastair', only 3.8 kms from this turn off. As it was only mid-afternoon, I drove past the gateway that supported the B&B sign, and continued on to see what the loch was like. On a sunny day I'm sure it would be more splendid, but even overcast, it was a very pretty area. There was even a patch of snow on the peaks of two fairly low-lying mountains nearby, and the black water in the loch was whipped up into choppy waves by the wind. At Kinloch Rannoch I drove slowly through the little township, which is comprised of a few shops and a petrol station, and here I stopped at a café. The road divided halfway through town, the left junction crossing an arched stone bridge over the runoff from the loch. Before I went in for any refreshments, I walked down to the water and took a short video of the rushing black water going through the three arches beneath.

When I arrived back at the café I found it was just closing, but they told me to try the hotel further down the road. Driving down toward the hotel, the loch opened up into a huge expanse of dark water, low lying hills with gently rounded peaks behind them, and shelly beaches. It is a popular place for fishing judging by the various 4-wheel drives and their loaded equipment that passed me on the road. At the hotel, I settled into a window seat in the bar area that overlooked the loch, and enjoyed a hearty beef and ale pie. I also took the opportunity, as I always did, to use the wifi to upload pictures to my blog.

By 7pm I retraced my journey along the road and turned in at the gate to see the small stone house just beside it. It hardly seemed worthy of the name 'The Gardens' but just before I got out my bags, a scruffy older man appeared at the front door and pointed further down the drive. All was explained.

Up and over a woody hill I drove and through a small glade of trees until the road opened out to reveal a two-storey stone house

set on emerald green lawns bedecked with daffodils. What? This was more my idea of Lallybroch! A carpark, a stone garage or barn, and in the distance a mountaintop on the other side of the loch. I parked and by the time I got out of the car, a spritely elderly man had emerged from the glass conservatory attached to the back of the house and introduced himself to me as Jim. He picked up the biggest case and led the way back into the conservatory and straight through a door in the middle and up a set of stairs. To my added delight, I was given half of the upper house to luxuriate in: separate bathroom, hallway, lounge area and a big yellow bedroom with a window straight out onto the mountain in the distance. All for the measly sum of £45!

I shared the floor with a regular guest I didn't meet until the morning, who had his own bedroom and ensuite on the other side. After writing in my diary with a comforting cup of tea and flicking through some of the tv channels, I went to bed and slept soundly until early morning.

Jenny Jeffries

Friday 22 May
Tummel Bridge to Carrbridge

The sky showed patches of blue at first glance from my window this Friday morning, and I looked forward to making my way up toward Inverness, stopping for the night well before getting there at a place called Carrbridge.

First, though, I was going to ask about the filming of Outlander in the area I was staying – which was part of the Trossachs. My host knew nothing about Outlander until he disappeared into the kitchen area to speak to his wife, whom I never met. It was she who apparently cooked my breakfast, and she who must watch the news and keep up with local events. The other guest, a fisherman, came downstairs and took his 'usual' table. We had a pleasant chat about New Zealand, the weather and fishing, and he provided me with the first Scottish saying appropriate to the season: "Never cast a clout, 'til May's out." (Don't put away your clothes until the end of May. Wise words indeed.)

When Jim joined us carrying breakfast, he was quite suddenly a mine of information about the Outlander filming in the area. He could even point me in the direction of where the filming of Claire and Frank going up to the stones had happened. There were no stones, of course, for they were cleverly magicked up by Starz, but the hills and the surrounding countryside were used in those scenes.

And so I turned left at the gates and went back to the stone bridge at Kinloch Rannoch. The road forked on the other side and – in keeping with my instructions – I kept left and took a zig-zagging road up to the top of the range of hills, where there was farm gate. Indeed, the countryside looked just like the area that a windswept Claire had woken dazedly to find herself back in time. I could picture Frank moving purposefully up the slope in search of her, and later, both Jamie and Claire climbing up to reach their watershed experience at the top. As for me, only a cluster of mute sheep observed my pleasure at the discovery of the famous setting. Tucking a dewy clump of long sheep wool into my pocket I went back to the car and retraced my journey. (The wool now graces the noticeboard in front of my desk).

On the way down to the bridge, with the road so narrow that the car crawled around the corners, a red deer startled me when it leapt across the road just ahead, and a black-faced ewe with two lambs scuttled in front of me along the road searching for a gap in the fence.

I passed the entrance to 'The Gardens' and then Tummel Bridge itself. When the narrow stream beside the road opened into the broad waters of Loch Tummel I stopped again at the famous viewing point called 'Queen's View', named appropriately after Queen Victoria who wrote about the place in her own diary: "Where we got out and took tea – 3rd October 1866." The viewing platform itself had a busload of elderly tourists leaning on the railing and taking snaps. I clicked a couple off and then hastened ahead of them back to the counter of the spacious tearooms, where I ordered cake and tea myself. The huge windows captured much of the view, but I enjoyed the quotes written along the walls as much: 'Sure by Tummel and Loch Rannoch and Lochaber I will go – The Road to the Isles'.

The Pass of Killicrankie is on the main road (A9) between Inverness and Edinburgh, and just north of the point where the road from Kinloch Rannoch comes out. It was here that a battle was fought between the clans supporting James VII and the troops supporting William of Orange on 27 July 1689. There is a very good information centre that I stopped to investigate, having everything on display from weapons used, to a model of a highlander with kilt dropped on ground as he runs into the fray(!), to beautifully detailed 3D models of moments during the battle. The story was outlined in chronological order throughout, and with the nearby mountains and gully so close, it was easy to imagine the actual event.

When I eased my car out onto the two-way road and continued north at speed (oh joy!) I was aware of the distance I wanted to cover today if I was to stop for the night just after Aviemore. Looking back, one of my regrets is that having reached Blair Castle, just a little distance from Killicrankie, I did not go in. I drove up the beautiful tree-lined drive until I reached the ticket office, seeing a hint now and then of the famously white walls of this castle through the gardens. Blair Castle is up the slopes from Blair Atholl village, and is the ancestral home of the Murray clan. A glance online at the website will assure you of the mistake I made in missing this fairy tale castle. Its glistening white walls and turrets glow starkly against the green of the trees and grassy slopes rising behind and around it. When I found out it cost £10.50 to go in, and I knew it would take the better part of two hours to do it justice, I turned tail and headed away. I had secretly hoped to be able to view the castle from the grounds, but they would not let me further than the gates.

Continuing on the A9, I reached Newtonmore after just under an hour, and my drive had followed the edges of the famous Cairngorms National Park. At Newtonmore is the Highland Folk

Museum, a portion of which was used in the filming of the episode 'Rent' in Outlander. Touted as 'Britain's first open air museum' this site is a mile long and features a wide range of different houses and crofts. I skimmed briskly through all the other crofts and workshops on disply and then set off through the woods for the 1700s township of six thatch-roofed houses.

Cresting the hill I had another of those thrills surge through me at the sight of something familiar straight off the screen. And as if waiting for me – ha! – a peasant woman spinning wool on a spindle with one hand, greeted me warmly at the brow of the hill, and we stopped to chat.

Of course, she knew all the details of what had been filmed there and where it took place. With that fresh knowledge in mind, I strode down past the pond where the table to collect rent had been set up, then where the wagon with Jamie twirling his knife had sat, then up to the wool-waulking area and in to the dim interior where the women had shared a drink. Naturally I set up my self-timer and crouched as if to pee in a wooden bucket, just like Claire. (Quite glad no one came along just then).

Being a bit lazy I took the offer of a ride in a enclosed metal carriage pulled behind a tractor to return to the carpark. I would have enjoyed conversation with the Australians and Scottish who joined me, but the squealing and shrieking of the metal panels as the carriage went over the rough ground precluded easy conversation. Some light refreshments at the café, and a browse of the shop, and then I was again on my way, this time east toward Aviemore.

Now I was in ski-resort country – or it would have been had there been snow. Instead there were plenty of outdoor adventurers driving through the centre of town, to find accommodation at one of the many lodges, or eat at the restaurants. I paid for my parking and then the restrooms before setting off for the Tourist Information Office, where I got a map and instructions about where in the Cairngorms Outlander had been filmed. That first episode when Claire is riding with Jamie and the others through wooded countryside, and maybe parts of 'Rent' when they are between villages on their horses with the wagon. This was Tulloch Ghru, featured in the opening credits. Driving in on the single-lane track following signs to the Tulloch Ghru and Black Park Road until I reached a car park, I stopped at a promontory and

got out to take in the vista ahead. The Cairngorms are vast! If I had expected to find a specific setting here in this broad expanse of valley, forest and distant mountain, I was disappointed. At least I knew I was in the right general area. I walked downhill until I came to the cycleway that wove extensively through this area, and which was particularly busy at this season. If I used my overworked imagination I could 'see' just where the horses would have been walking. I stood for a while on the empty cycleway looking to where the path disappeared into woods, and felt a longing to be wheeling my way along it. Next time, perhaps. If I set out walking off the path and deeper in to the valley, I feel sure I'd never be heard from again – it looked that extensive and wild.

Up I walked to the car park and back to the safe confines of my car, and a last contemplation of the scene ahead as the breeze whipped up and I felt a shiver take me. It was certainly not summer yet.

Carrbridge is a town just beyond Aviemore, and less 'touristy' with old stone buildings and a pub or two. I was staying at Craigellachie Guesthouse on the main street, in a compact single room with ensuite for £40. It had a little triangular bathroom, and bedroom large enough to fit a single bed but no room to open a case on the floor. It was cosy and very clean and really that was all that mattered.

Dinner was a couple of doors down the street at a pub, and when I opened the doors the noise was deafening and I had to squeeze through the crowd to reach the relatively quiet restaurant beyond. I uploaded pictures to the blog, and checked emails, and ate a homecooked meal (that I cannot recall now) before I headed back to my tiny room.

Saturday 23 May

Carrbridge to Culloden

Culloden Moor is only half an hour from Carrbridge, taking the A9 toward Inverness and turning off on the A96. It was relatively flat countryside but undulating and dotted with stands of trees and scrub. The sky was a brilliant blue and I was humming as I drove past the entrance to the Culloden Moor and Information Centre. I thought I might as well go and see a bit further along this coastline if I was returning to spend the night at Culloden House.

Another fifteen minutes along the road a signpost to Cawdor Castle caught my eye. Heck, can you see too many castles? And after all, I had just missed Blair Castle the previous day.

The fresh green spring growth was dazzling against the blue sky in the arch of trees overhead as I rounded the corner and found the car park. Birds sang, cicadas thrummed. . . oh, wait, this isn't a Disney story. . . sorry. It DID feel a bit like one though. There was a gypsy caravan under a laden blossom tree, begging for investigation. An ice cream parlour beside it served coffee as well, and dotted out on the grassy lawn under the trees were ornate iron tables and chairs. All it lacked was a bright blue bird perching on my shoulding and chirping, 'Somewhere over the rainbow'. The path led on to the bridge over a moat into this elegant but modest castle. I decided to look through the castle first and return for coffee there later.

This castle has been home to the Cawdor family for over 600 years, and is still occupied by one of them. The rooms are full of furnishings and paintings, tapestries and many small items of interest. Despite every attempt to make it 'homey', I couldn't help but feel it would be a cold, drafty sort of place to inhabit. We were not allowed to take photographs inside which I found particularly taxing when I got to the splendid basement and kitchen area, where an old well is sunk in the ground, and from which they used to draw water. (I just love discovering things like that, and usually find the commonplace parts of a castle the more interesting). I'd as soon go through a furnished croft smelling of peat and furnished with box beds, as up the spiral staircase of one of these dwellings. In the basement, just before we were guided by arrows and notices into the shop, I saw two ancient bicycles, and somehow my finger slipped and a couple of photos were taken.

Outside, the extensive gardens were beckoning and the day so gorgeous that I walked slowly around enjoying them. There was a hedged maze surrounded by a tree-lined bower, used extensively in period dramas when princesses receive advice from their royal parent. For once, the shadows played strongly on the ground ahead, and I walked through them to the next symmetrical arrangement. This was a topiary garden with box hedges and herbaceous borders dotted now and then with a fountain or statue.

In the tidy orchard, resplendent with white blossom trees, I lay on the grass looking up at the sky and felt sublimely happy. From the far corner of the garden looking back up at the castle turrets, I marvelled at how amazing it was to be right there, in a scene from a fairy tale. I had my coffee outside at the wrought iron tables . . . and then drove back towards Culloden.

The scenery gradually changed. No longer were there tall trees and cropped lawns in rolling countryside, I was now heading on to a heather-covered moor, where the wind often sweeps across the low fields and the prospect is wild and bleak. Certainly the history surrounding Culloden is more the stuff of nightmares, than fairytales. As I approached the turn off for Culloden Information Centre, I passed a sign for the Clava Stones, and another bell went off in my head. I turned the car and took this five-minute diversion down behind the Culloden Battlefield to a car park set among trees. Getting out, I could see a fenced off field in which various stones mounds and circles of stones jutted up and briskly made my

way across to them. I had no idea they were so extensive. In fact, I actually thought they were 'just' a ring of stones, but there were cairns here as well, all dating from the Bronze Age. There are three rings of cairns – a carefully built circular mound of rocks used for burial – as well as a few standing stone arrangements around them. It is hard to get a sense of the age of these arrangements of stone as you stand in the middle of something that took a lot of men a long time to put together, for some unknown reason, way back in the day.

Naturally, on this my first time at some standing stones in Scotland, I set up my I-pad and took a photo with [12]my hand reaching out to touch one of the largest. I would have lingered longer but a bus arrived in the car park, and near me, there was a noisy altercation between some tourists arguing with someone who had put a rock in his pocket. Tempted though I was to join the fray – who takes a bit of history away with them like that!? – instead I left and drove the short distance up to the Culloden Battlefield car park (pay and display of course). It was a day for picking one's fights.

As I walked the paved pathway to the sliding doors, I walked over paving stones carved with the names of many who had contributed to the centre, and there, sure enough, was one: 'In honor of Diana Gabaldon from Ladies of Lallybroch'.

The Visitor Centre is a large modern building that has an excellent display of the chronology of the battle, the politics behind it, and various interactive areas where it is possible to hear or see from the people who were involved. It is well worth the £11 entry. A glance at the website will give you all you need to know about the experience inside, and there is also a well stocked and run café and shop. On this, my second visit, I had much more time to go at my own speed through the various display halls, listening and watching the story unfold. (Previously I was part of a tour group who had only an hour on site).

12. In the story 'Outlander', Claire finds herself back in 1743 after touching some standing stones.

At the end of the displays in the centre of a room is a flat diorama around which you stand to observe the battle played out in detail. It is particularly chilling to watch the action unfold in miniature and the little human figures fall like so many dominos before the artillery or sword, and leaves a lasting impression. With those images still in mind, I stepped out onto the moor itself.

What greeted me just outside the door was a 'real' Highlander clad in a cornucopia of garish tartans, with a blue bonnet and broadsword. He posed with me, letting me hold the gun, but sadly, the fact that I towered over him somewhat destroyed the impression of fearsome warrior he might have been attempting to achieve.

I wandered soberly around the markers in silence. When I reached the big stone memorial I sat for a while staring out at the bleak field, trying to imagine how the Highlanders found the strength to run, starving as they were, in kilts and carrying heavy weapons, over the uneven and scrubby ground into gun and cannon fire.

Looking out to my right was the Fraser stone – familiar through the many photos online taken by Outlanders on pilgrimage to locations in the books. I was just another pilgrim to this particular place and stone. I had in my pocket a piece of quartz from Thames coastline, in New Zealand, and managed to squeeze it down beside the Fraser stone. (I'm sure it would be gone the next time a weed-eater goes through the area). The next part of my 'ritual' was to take a drink of whisky from my new flask, and pour a little on the stone, with a "Slainte mhath" uttered softly. This I did with a furtive glance around to see who might be watching. The windy plain marked with stone memorials and two lines of flags showing the positions of the Red Coats and the Highlanders, begs a moment or two of solemn reflection. Without going into the details of the battle and the story behind it, it is sad enough to know that it marked the end of the clans as they were known up until then. In my own family, there is both Dickinson and Urquhart

blood, and both these forebears left Scotland around this time, to eventually end up in Australia and New Zealand. It was my plan to go to the Black Isle on the next day, and there see what I could discover of the Urquhart line.

What follows next is a real highlight of my trip. When planning my journey I had bantered back and forth with a Californian Twitter friend called Robert Wealleans, whom I've never met. He put up a photo of Culloden House and commented that it needed to be part of my itinerary. I replied that it was well beyond my budget. In response, he insisted on paying a sizeable amount into my Paypal account to make that night possible. I was astounded at his generosity, and naturally, thrilled! Then another Kiwi friend, Rhonnie Brinsdon, who had already made my corset and shift for me free of charge, arranged with Culloden House to pay for my dinner! I was and still am, deeply humbled by their generosity and kindness. Culloden House began following me on Twitter and said there would be a surprise upon my arrival. Imagine my excitement as I turned my car up the long drive that leads up to this palatial hotel at around 4pm on this day.

I walked up the ballastraded steps, through the main door, and checked in at the main desk where a man wearing the colours of the house smilingly welcomed me, and handed my keys to a porter. This man set off towards my humble little VW Polo to get my bags. After all the formalities of registration were completed, I was led up the gracious curving stairway to the first floor and through doors and hallway to a large polished wooden door with 'Room 15' on its plate. Upon being ushered in to the sitting room of this apartment, I was told it was the room that Diana Gabaldon stayed in when she came. I had been upgraded to Herself's own room!

This was no modern, neutrally stylish hotel, but an opulent, comfortable, friendly house, full of character and old world charm. Through my door was a sitting room with sofas and television, and

Diana Gabaldon
From
The Ladies of the Lallybroch
2011

a table with a welcome tray of fruit and chocolates. In the bedroom a four poster king-sized bed with quilted covers and cushions, writing desk, dressing table, and the bathroom had a deep bath and tiled floor. I rolled around on the bed for a while just luxuriating before going downstairs to take a stroll around the gardens.

I found the walled garden, and let myself in, to walk its perimeter until I found the 'Diana Gabaldon' seat, donated by the Ladies of the Lallybroch in 2011. Naturally I took a selfie sitting in it, imagining Diana having done the same numerous times. (Not taking a selfie, sitting in it!) When I tweeted the picture later, she responded with a warm: "Sit in good health"!

Back in my room, I shook out the best clothes I could find in my small suitcase, and sat at the dressing table trying to refine my look for a formal dinner. Somewhat nervously I descended the stairs, and, having never been in a 'whisky room' took advantage of the offer and joined a few others seated in wing back chairs sipping on their drinks. I let the waiter choose for me, and my glow of happiness at being there was further heightened by the glow in my cheeks as the whisky 'took hold'. The cabinet from which he selected my whisky was laden with more bottles of the Scottish spirit than I've seen in one place.

When I made my way through to the dining room, it was like stepping in to a scene from Downton Abbey: chandeliers, burgundy wallpaper with embossed golden crests on it, white linen tablecloths and crockery with an edging of gold. My own table was set out for me, and beside the flowers was a card that simply stated, 'Enjoy your stay, Jenny – Robert'. When I asked for a glass of merlot, the whole bottle was left, another gift from Robert.

The food was delectable, served in deliciously dainty portions arranged artfully on my plate – pigeon, lamb, spring vegetables, sauces. I savoured every mouthful of this finest meal I would have in Scotland. Afterwards, I was given the bottle to take, and offered a complimentary brandy in the 'whisky room'. (I'm glad I was not

driving afterwards). Back upstairs, I made myself a cup of tea in the sitting room and lingered there before disappearing into the soft depths of the bed. My last thoughts: how strange to be sleeping in the same bed that the author of these stories has drifted off in her own dreams in.

Sunday 24 May
Culloden to Beauly

I lingered as long as I could in my luxurious bed this morning, and had a deep relaxing bath, before going down to a sumptious a la carte breakfast of smoked fish.

Today I would be meeting a group of Inverness Outlanders at the café at Culloden Battlefield for lunch. Having an hour to fill before meeting them, I drove 20 minutes on the A96 to the seaside town of Nairn for a look at the North Sea and the place where the Duke of Cumberland ('The Butcher') slept on the night before the battle on 16 April 1746. On a sunny summer day I imagine Nairn is busy and popular, but today the wind blew in gusts and it threatened rain. I stepped out on to the pale sands and admired the view out toward the Black Isle.

I was early at the café at Culloden site, first to await the Inverness Outlanders, and not sure how many would come. In the next ten minutes I was joined at my table by four beaming lasses, some of the faces I already recognised from the Gathering. During the course of our merry lunch together, in discussing where I was off to next, Angie offered a room at her house outside Beauly for the coming night. Not for the first time or last time, I had cause to be grateful to be part of such a generous fan group.

My first destination was Cromarty on the Black Isle (this is not actually an island, but a peninsula). It was here that the Urquharts had been based, and the genealogical chart of my family had 'Ross and Cromarty' as the origin of my earliest known ancestors. I drove straight through Inverness without stopping, and then out through the middle of the Isle to reach Cromarty at the furthest point. This was undulating but relatively flat land, dotted with farms, pastures, and a pretty village or two, and I passed them enjoying the sense of my forbears having known this land intimately.

When I reached Cromarty, I parked and walked up and

down the curved streets of this fishing village, taking in the old stone or brick buildings, two storeyed and all bearing the stamp of ancient use. In a very busy café called 'The Pantry' I squeezed in through the door, eased past the occupied tables and found one available place to sit and have lunch. I remember thinking as I swallowed my slightly dry cake, that they could do with more cafes in the UK in general. The few good ones I found were always so busy that the staff looked harried – as these did – and the service was rushed. Still, nothing dampened my joy at being in the place of my forbears, and after eating I followed a signpost pointing to an information centre and went up the road toward the old brick courthouse.

At the entrance to the museum was a poster – a long-winded equivalent to 'The Urquharts Aren't Home', which I still chuckle about to this day. Entitled 'Urquharts and Cromarty' with a subtitle stating 'Scattered across the world' – it was an elaborate chart pointing out the movements of the clan away from their land to dispersal throughout the world. Well, I could have told them that! It points out that the clan chieftain lives in New Orleans, and all the various reasons why and how the clan dispersed for a better life elsewhere. There are very few Urquharts left in Cromarty now.

I particularly enjoyed the courtroom drama set up in a room upstairs. When I opened the door, mechanisms slid into place and voices issued forth from models set up on the bench and in the dock. I slipped into the back and enjoyed hearing the 'trial'. Afterwards I walked around the graveyard behind church next door, and stepped in to the ancient ruins of the Old Gaelic Chapel up the hill, where I uttered a simple prayer in the silence – sadly, not in gaelic.

Driving back towards Dingwall along the upper coastal road, I was astounded at the rows of oil rigs staggered out along the Cromarty Firth, all there for construction or repair. They make an impressive sight. Looking North across the Firth, the photos I

took have a surreal quality: rich blue sky with white clouds dancing across it, the green of pasture and brilliant yellow of the fields of rapeseed, and between it all, that long grey finger of the sea. Far off on the horizon were rounded mountains with patches of snow on their peaks. I didn't know it, but once I went over to the west of the Highlands, this pastoral idyll would be exchanged for the wild windy greyness of that more rugged area.

To my added delight, there was a long bridge that crossed the Firth and from there Dingwall is but a short drive west. Nearly thirty years ago I stopped at Dingwall having travelled up on the train, and it was there that I saw the name Urquhart on many of the gravestones. I always wanted to come back and investigate further.

Beauly ('beautiful place') was only a short drive through the countryside from Dingwall. I had been here two and a half years ago  in the heart of winter, when snow made the ruins of the priory even more stark. This ancient priory, founded in 1230, is at the centre of this town, and for those of us who are Outlander fans, the enigmatic figure of Simon Lovat Fraser is interwoven in its history. Here, the names Fraser and Mackenzie can be seen on monuments and gravestones. This is country that is written into the book series, and an historic figure who is written up as the fictional Jamie Fraser's grandfather. The area has known lively political action, and is the setting for many battles particularly during the Jacobite rising. Simon 'the Fox' Fraser – so called for the crafty way he preserved his clan through the playing of both sides in the Jacobite rising, and his unorthodox methods of getting what he wanted.

Beside the Priory, in the central square of Beauly, is a large carpark where tour buses can pull in and let their passengers disembark into the nearby hotels and restaurants. I pulled in beside them and ambled through thePriory first, enjoying the totally different spring appearance of the park, with blossom and daffodils in place of snow. The town is not large, and did not take long to explore, and I soon found a comfortable chair in a hotel nearby, where I used the wifi and had coffee. Angie, the Inverness Outlander who had offered to have me stay overnight, had suggested she meet me and drive ahead of me to their house, which was more difficult to find. We met and hugged, as if we'd known each other some time, and then meandered out of town until we stopped at the large house that was their home. Here I was offered a guest room with queen bed and ensuite, and a window overlooking the valley I had just driven up. I met Charles, Angie's husband, and the two grey and white cats called Bubble and Squeak. After nearly a week driving around by myself since the hectic 'Gathering' the previous weekend, it was bliss to relax at a kitchen table, while food was prepared around me, and the conversation constant and lively. We ate a homemade and hearty fish pie made up of prawns and three different sorts of fish, with mashed spuds and cheese melted over it. Comfort food at its highest. While Bubble stared at me without blinking from a neighbouring chair, Charles chatted on almost every subject you can imagine. His astuteness being matched by a growing woolliness in my own brain function, and it is a credit to his hospitality that neither he nor Angie made me feel the least bit thick-headed. It may have been exacerbated by the presence of two bottles of whisky that sat on the table between us, my glass refilled a couple of times until I could pick the difference between a peaty one and the non-smoky. They both knew their whisky well, and I was able to impress them with my photo of the whisky room trolley at Culloden House. Eventually I made my way to bed and was asleep in seconds.

Monday 25 May
Beauly to Glenelg

Angie was gone when I arose, and so I roamed the kitchen with Charles and made toast to go with my tea.

When I'd been at lunch with the Inverness Outlanders I'd heard about the [13]Wardlaw Mausoleum, just up the hill from where I was, at Kirkhill. Angie had reiterated how worthwhile it would be to go and see the place where The Old Fox himself was interred. Apparently there was a man called Eric who lived nearby, who would probably show me around if I called him and asked. I did so. I drove up the country lanes until I approached a village on a hill, and even as I began my drive into the outer fringes of the town, noticed the first road on the left pointed to 'Wardlaw Mausoleum'. Being a little early, I wandered around the graveyard looking at the gravestones that surrounded a cute little 'mini-church' complete with bell tower. Before long a tall grey-bearded chap clutching a cardboard box full of books approached me and introduced himself. He was, indeed, Eric, and I was about to have an experience I still talk about whenever I discuss my Scotland adventure. Eric led me into the Mausoleum, and put his box down on the windowsill. His first question: "How long have you got?" and my response: "Why don't you just start."

So began about an hour of a fascinating personal lecture, as he showed me around the various Frasers mentioned in the memorials along the wall. Eric is a born storyteller, and I wished there had been more than just me standing there (you'll recall my experience just the night before, being the least agile-minded of the party). By the time we had worked our way around to the Old Fox himself, and checked out some of the pictures and engravings in the books Eric had brought with him, I was quite ready to go and see the lead coffin that housed old Lovat Fraser's headless corpse. (That is another story – to do with a beheading at the Tower of

13. Refer www.wardlawmausoleum.com The restoration of this Mausoleum and its upkeep is dependant upon donations and volunteers, and I strongly urge any with an interest in Scottish history to check out the website link and support them.

London after Culloden, and collapsing scaffolding, and the phrase: "Laughed his head off" referring to Lovett Fraser watching about sixteen people die just before his own life was taken.)

At this point, Eric put down the book he was holding and walked to a heavy wooden door set into the floor of the building and locked with a metal latch. Unlocking it, he stood to one side and bending down took hold of a solid metal ring, indicating to me that I should do likewise on the other side. It took two of us to lever the door up and prop it against the wall, and he needed to hold it in place. From where I stood I saw a narrow set of stairs leading down into the crypt below, and about five old warped coffins filling that small space.

It did cross my mind as I descended alone into the depths clutching my camera nervously, that I did not know Eric all that well.

These were the quickest snapshots I've ever taken, and mere seconds later I was ascending up into the light toward the grinning face above.

I had barely recovered my equilibrium when we walked outside and Eric asked if I'd like to ring the bell. Naturally, after that hasty cowardly return from the depths of the crypt, I needed to sound assertive and confident again, and so I agreed. Rounding the corner, he opened the tiny door leading into the bell tower and indicated the narrow winding plaster stairway, leading up in a tight curve around plaster walls. He would stay below.

I was wearing black jeans and black jacket and my long hair newly washed was trailing down my back 'drying'. If anyone can remember the picture of Winnie the Pooh stuck in the rabbit hole, you'll come close to realising my predicament. I felt both sides of the narrow space as I made my way at a crawl up the uneven steps, afraid at any minute to become wedged forever in there. After three circuits, there was an opening ahead and the rope of the bell hanging loose above me. My heart was beating in time with the

bell as I wrenched heavily on it and rang it three times. Then I clambered backwards down the steps, leaving strands of golden hair clinging to the walls in my speed to get out. I must have popped like a pimple out into the light, covered in plaster dust and looking a little red. It has made a great story since then.

Now began my real foray into the wilds of the Highlands!

I was going to travel today from the eastern shores of Scotland directly across to the western shores. My intention was to avoid the usual route along the lochs between Inverness and the Kyle of Lochalsh and go on the northern route through Garve and down through the Wester Ross mountains (A832 and A890).

It took a good hour and a half to drive in this arc through to the west, and as I drove I noticed the mountains increasing, and the clouds growing darker. It was quite beautiful and certainly more remote to drive through than the more popular way further south. By the time I was on the A890 heading south, the road was narrower, but the scenery spectacular with small lochs and rivers. To my left was a deepening gorge that was filled with the dark waters of Loch Monar. Little white houses with slate roofs were dotted here and there on the foothills.

By 1.30pm I had descended from the hilly road to a T-junction onto the main highway leading to the Kyle of Lochalsh, but instead of turning right, I turned left to go and see the castle at Eilean Donan first. Despite the number of times I've seen this picturesque setting in almost every tourist site for Scotland, it did not disappoint. Even on this grey day, the sight of the castle and its three-arched bridge leading out towards it, reflected in the water of Loch Duich, was breath-taking. Of course, I was shoulder to shoulder with a lot of other people snapping shots of the castle on their cameras too, and the car park was full, tour buses were turning, and families dodged back and forth between café and toilets. I did not linger. I wrote down a few accommodation places in my notebook, and then turned my car in the direction of Shiel

Bridge, which leads over to the other side of the loch, and up steeply into the mountains.

One of the places I'd been encouraged to go and see, and whose name I had written in my book, was Glenelg – a pretty little town on the southern side of the mountain, which faced out upon the Isle of Skye. When I left the main road and crossed the bridge I was in single-lane territory again, and not just a narrow road but a winding and steep one! Eventually I would get used to these, but it was early days. Up and up my little black car wound, ducking occasionally into a passing bay as another car approached, until I saw a larger parking area and the words 'Look Out Point'.

It is very odd to step out and gaze in rapture at a wide vista that seems faintly familiar – as if in a dream - and then realise you've seen it before, but in its winter clothes. Yes, indeed, the little minibus tour I'd taken in December two and half years earlier had wound up that same hill and stopped here. Back then, the mountains were white, and glistening in a pale blue sky, and the loch looked black. Now the scene was all greens, mustards, navy, and ochre, and the heavy clouds scudded over it all in restless patterns on an azure sky. I just loved it. An engraved notice on a plinth pointed out features of the landscape ahead, like the 'five sisters' – mountain peaks that would appear a few times on my travels in the area.

My car rattled over the brow of the hill and down into a valley, past the odd farm with a white croft house and buildings, stone fences, and assorted livestock. The road wound into a little group of ancient shops and houses, and at the end, a sign and driveway leading down into a cosy pub called 'The Glenelg Inn' whose car park looked surprisingly full. My enquiry about a room met with incredulity and a flat, 'No' from the manager. Nothing daunted, I strode across the road and into the general store, to ask about accommodation for the night. That kindly woman got out a pen and paper and jotted a few numbers down, offering it to me with a smile. When I got back to my car to make the calls, I

discovered I had no signal with which to make calls on my phone!

Still confident, I drove along the coast enjoying the view over the water to what I would later discover to be the shoreline of Skye. The beach was pebbly and full of driftwood and rocks and the houses along this stretch of road mostly small single-level dwellings, white with dark roofs. I stopped outside a house with 'Marabhaig Bed & Breakfast' on a signpost by the gate and knocked. A cheerful blonde woman, who seemed taken aback at my enquiry, checked her register and then reluctantly agreed for the sum of around £40. Perhaps I looked like I'd be no trouble. As I never saw any other guests it must have been for the reasons she disclosed over breakfast later: that she was crossing to Lewis at any moment should her aunty 'pass away'. As you can see, Margaret Cameron and I were disclosing information about our families and homes within quite a short while. She was astounded to discover I intended to go to Skye the next few days and had not booked one night. "I doubt you'll find any place that can take you now – it's always popular. I'll give you a number to call." Once I was shown my room, which had the amazing addition of a shower cubicle standing alone in the corner, I spent the next hour calling every accommodation place on Skye (my phone worked now that I had a signal). To my great relief, I secured three different places on the island for the next three nights.

Pleased to have my accommodation for Skye settled, I thought I'd use the remaining afternoon to go and see the brochs that were further along the road. These are Dun Telve and Dun Troddan and are over 2,000 years old, dating from the Iron Age. Coming as I do from a relatively young country, you can only imagine the sensations as I approached along a narrow country lane and saw to my right a tall rock structure set back among some trees. I really knew I was in a place that was rooted in long history. I passed through the gate and approached this 10m high tower, seeing the narrow door leading in. One or two others were wandering around inside, but all I noticed were the passageways between the walls, the evidence of stairs and of struts for different levels, and the amazing precision used in building a double-walled drystone structure of this size. Unfortunately a large portion of the broch was missing, no doubt the stone used for other construction over the years, but a helpful poster showed what it would have looked like.

Just a little further along the road, and on the left, is a path up to the second broch, which is better preserved. From this vantage point it was possible to look down along the valley and see Broch Telve in the distance. No one knows why these two brochs were built so close together, but their proximity means you get double value for the effort in going to see them. It occurred to me, as I stood inside the walls of the second broch and looked out, that much of the ancient world (of which Scotland has in abundance) would never have survived in New Zealand, which suffers so many earthquakes.

It was time to go and seek a place for dinner, so I drove back in to Glenelg, certain I'd find a welcome at the inn for food at least. Once more, I was disappointed. Not only was I turned away, but in such a gruff and offhand way I am mentioning it in this story. I'm sure they were busy, but at the time there were plenty of tables, and they did not even ascertain whether I would be long or need much. It's a shame they were the only place serving food in town.

I returned to my room and sorted through my car and my possessions for what food I had on hand. (Yes, I always have food 'on hand', and agreed, it was not as if I couldn't do with a brief fast!) As it happened, I had some ginger loaf, an orange, and a cup of tea – and so passed the only evening I did not have a 'proper' dinner in my entire trip. Later, Margaret knocked on my door, and stood chatting in the doorframe for a while. She was shocked at the inhospitality of the Inn, but not surprised, and offered me some cheese on toast or something, which I turned down.

It was still as bright as midday when I finished writing in my diary and turned off the light.

126

Tuesday 26 May
Glenelg to Torrin, Skye

I took some delight in the whimsical nature of the road as it meandered up and out of Glenelg the next morning. Narrow one moment, it would gradually broaden to two-lane briefly before narrowing again and providing a passing bay every now and then. I'd had a sturdy breakfast alone in the dining room, facing a ticking grandfather clock and sitting on one of a number of antique chairs. Margaret was particularly keen to set me up on Lewis in the Outer Hebrides at a cousin's hostel for my accommodation, so I took the number down in my notebook. She thought she might be nearby herself, attending her aunt's funeral.

The brochs at Glenelg

I'd seen the ferry to Skye pass in front of the house in the morning, the very one my friend and I must have used when we'd crossed to the island in 1989 before the bridge was built. On the top of the hill at the lookout point, I took another photo of the five sisters – with low lying grey cloud and the waters steely and choppy.

This time when I reached the main road I drove past Eilean Donan castle without stopping. It was almost a relief to be able to drive reasonably fast and I reached the Kyle of Lochalsh by 9.30am. Even on this grey rainy day, the wonderful long span of the bridge to Skye was worth stopping to see and recording. On my previous trip in the minibus tour, our driver had made us all get out and walk across the bridge – in December, in the snow. I had a deep appreciation for its length and height, and the stunning views all around. There to the left as I approached the coastline of Skye, was the pretty little township of Kyleakin, where I've stayed twice before: once in 1989, fresh off the ferry, and again in 2012 on the minibus tour. It was cheap and friendly and a place of fishermen, backpackers and day-trippers.

I felt a surge of excitement when I drove off the bridge onto Skye, and was humming the Skye Boat song as I did. Although my GPS was not working, I had a map of the island and had marked the places I was staying for the night. Some uncertainty assailed me as I considered the addresses I was to use, which I am sure would not have worked on the Google Maps application anyway: 'Slapin View, Torrin, Broadford', 'Uiginish Farmhouse, Dunvegan'. Not a number in sight. I could see Torrin written in small blue letters on what looked a very minor road leading out of Broadford, and so I turned along it.

If I did not know better, I would have thought myself on a private drive. It was yet another narrow one-lane road, with passing bays and black-faced sheep and lambs roaming around nearby. There were distant mountains forming a backdrop to the rolling heather-covered hills nearby, and a swampy lake with reeds along

its bank. There was a moment when the white houses seemed to appear more often, and I had almost passed a drive with a sign saying 'Slapin View' so intent was I at the view ahead. I realised I must be in Torrin.

I drew up into the wee car park beside this two-storey croft house, with its requisite three windows along the top and two below with a door in the middle. I looked around and realised it was indeed a 'slapping view' – but thought it an odd house name. Upon my knock, an elderly and rather bent white-haired lady answered, looking up at me in some surprise. It was only 10.30am after all.

I explained that I was the Jenny who had called the night before, and only wanted to drop my bags off. She immediately smiled, although I have a feeling she struggled to understand my garbled words and accent. Up the central stairs I toted my two bags and in to a pretty gabled room on the right, with blue walls and gingham curtains at the little window. There was a queen bed made up, and a tray with kettle and tea things on the side table. Apparently the bathroom was shared and under the main stairs. I was told another couple would be coming for the night, and I assumed the central small room upstairs must be Mrs A's, my host. She made her way carefully down the stairs chatting in a warbling way until we reached the door. There we parted on great terms and I headed out for a day's adventure.

At the very end of this winding little road is a place called Elgol, featuring a café, and a few other buildings, as well as a couple of car parks. I had every intention of getting some walking done in Scotland, and had my boots and coat ready in the car. When I parked here I could see quite a number of people moving around in sturdy boots and carrying poles and the like, and making use of the 'facilities.' Sadly, the café was closed. Fortunately I had the huge thermos given me by Fiona in Edinburgh, and filled with tea from the B&B at Glenelg this morning. The tea was still hot and I had various half consumed packets of biscuits and other food items in the glove box – my 'refrigerator'. I sat in the car looking out on the bay down the steep slope in front of me, where the road wound down to the second car park. It, too, was full. Amazingly, large campervans negotiated these narrow windy roads, arriving at pokey little places like this where they were forced to turn somewhere or find parking. One was lumbering down toward us even now, and I decided to move on while I could. It was cold, windy and occasional showers blustered over – not weather I enjoyed hiking in. The guilt at my laziness stayed with me though, for much of my return towards Torrin, and when I saw a smaller car park beside a pretty loch, and a sign pointing to a walkway, I relented and parked the car. I dug out my boots, coat, and backpack, stuffing various items into it, along with my camera. I had every intention of walking for miles! Every intention – you see that don't you?

A family of five and their dog were ahead of me, bounding along a dirt path worn in the heather beside the loch edge. I stooped and took the photo that would support my bucket list point: 'Washed hands in a loch'. The little loch widened and I saw the family up ahead had stopped and were playing at the waters edge, so I smiled at them and pushed through, bracing myself for a sturdy hike.

About ten steps past them the path completely petered out, and, bewildered, I hunted for it. I found myself pushing through soggy heather, squelching in the marshy ground, and never getting a firm foothold. I went uphill and it all looked the same. I stood still and considered my options.

It was obvious that this was a way many 'real' hikers took because I'd seen some in the distance earlier. The sort who carried packs and had long poles and hats pulled close about their heads. Going on over this scrubby ground, I could see some sturdy peaks ahead and challenging terrain. How good it would feel at the end of a day of surmounting such obstacles, to finally pull wet gear off and cosy up in a tavern for dinner, knowing you'd walked the land like that! That feeling would remain foreign to me: I turned and

An Lùib
Luib 3.4m
Scottish Rights of Way and Access Society, Edin

Na Torran
Torran 1.2m
Scottish Rights of Way and Access Society, Edinbu

retraced my steps, pulling off my coat and boots at the car, and easing behind the wheel with a happy sigh. I didn't need to walk them to enjoy the mountains round about. They seemed to me to be like huge sleeping beasts, brown and furry, with a sprinkle of bright yellow gorse, dusky heather and an abundance of deep brackish black lochs.

I wove in and out of parking bays all the way back to Broadford, letting a lot of traffic go by on its way to . . . where? Elgol? At Broadford I turned south toward Kyleakin, but at the roundabout this side of the bridge took the second exit and headed out along the southern edge of Skye toward Armadale and the castle belonging to clan Donald. This road was a two-lane and well sealed, so I made it to the end in good time enjoying the views out over the Sound of Sleat (you've got to love Scottish place names!)

When I reached Armadale I stocked up at the local store, and then drove to overlook the water, feeling suddenly quite tired. Lying my seat back, I closed my eyes and drifted off for about half an hour. It was therefore about 4pm when I arrived at the castle to do the tour of the gardens. My plans changed with the discovery that the cost to roam around was £8.50 and with the day still wet and windy, I didn't want to spend the money for a mere hour in the gardens and so I just looked around the shop and info centre. Then I returned to my car and drove out along a winding single-lane to Ord, on the northern edge of this peninsula. The scenery on this side was particularly dramatic, being a wide view of the sea with the distant Cuillin Hills of Skye visible across the water, and the clouds whipping across the blue sky. As I drove along to the coast I passed shallow pools emerging from low-lying cloud, the tussock grass yellow, dotted with burgundy heather, and spots of lime green spring grass. It made for a very textural effect and I knew I would want to paint these scenes upon my return.

My heart went in to my throat when I passed a sign that said 'filming in progress' as I drove down to a settlement near the water. There over by the rocks a group of people were clustered, holding lighting screens and other film equipment. Could it be? It seemed a long way for the Outlander crew to have come but I guess it was possible. Was I at last fated to meet with some of my beloved stars? I drove as close as I could and stopped to watch from the road. There were white vans and vehicles parked along side the road, and hope swelled within me. Then a lanky young man wearing a vest and walkie-talkie walked past my open window and I hailed him. He came closer and smiled at my question regarding the film: "It's a Gaelic film called 'Bannan'" he supplied. I hid my disappointment well. "Will I see it out in New Zealand?" "You may do, but it's unlikely," he responded. Then he loped off toward the group clustered down by the rocks.

Disappointed I turned right and followed the coast down toward the ruins of Castle Ord, which were marked on the map I held. There was a little clump of stone out on one of the promontories that I presume were the remains of the castle. I took some photos of the backdrop of navy mountains lost in cloud, the choppy seas, and the rugged coastline I was winding down through, and then turned inland to meet the main road again.

It was 5.15pm when I arrived back at the busy township of Broadford, and I was spoiled for choice regarding places to eat. Although it was quite early for dinner, I knew I could do with a relaxing drink looking out at the sea, and so made my way in to a promising-sounding place called Scottishly: 'The Claymore.' Sure enough, there was a friendly bar lit with golden light from the bay outside, some locals leaning over it chatting, and a comfortable spot to sit and use the wifi. I sipped my cider and settled in for the long haul: got my blog post uploaded, answered Facebook and Twitter posts, and grew hungrier. I was moved to a table near the window in the restaurant where I chose a local dish called 'Stumpy Lobster' for the main. This proved to be less like lobster and more like king prawn, and swimming in butter, but was comfort food never the less. I followed it with Sticky Toffee Pudding, which is also a regular on dessert menus in the UK, and felt quite replete.

The sun had actually drifted low enough to the horizon that it was through a golden light I drove back towards Torrin, passing a few groups of photographers all set up to capture that same light among the reeds and banks of the moor and loch, the dark brooding shape of the mountains behind.

When I unlatched the door to 'Slapin View', Mrs A emerged from her own living area to beckon me in for a cup of tea. The following hour was one of my finest in my whole journey around Scotland. In stark contrast to the other particularly fine night, at Culloden House, this was almost the opposite in terms of luxury, but equally rich in the warmth of the experience. In what once was the kitchen and dining area, my gregarious elderly landlady had created her own living space, complete with wood-fire stove, about four stuffed armchairs, and all the accoutrements of a kitchen. The air was redolent with peat, which was the fuel being burned, the last aroma of a hearty meal still lingered, and I eased back in one of the armchairs, loving the opportunity for a bit of natter. Mrs A relaxed in the stuffed chair beside me and talked about the tax that was taken from the pension given her after her husband's death some 26 years ago, and the 'roof tax' that all who own B&B's are saddled with. How much she likes the opportunity to meet people from all over the world. I learned her son lives across the road in one of the houses down there, and is single, and "I hope he never marries, he'd be terrible to live with!" I heard all about the family and her two granddaughters, and how her husband had died so long ago. There was a tale about a cow about to calve, that broke through a fence and got stuck at the top of the croft. The calf came, but the poor cow lost most of her 'parts' as well, until the vet came and sewed them all up again and the cow made a full recovery! I found out that the cattle belonged to her croft estate, but that all the black-faced sheep and lambs I passed on my way through were communally owned by the whole village – about 30 houses. For my part, I told her about New Zealand, and my life there. I showed her pictures on my I-pad of home and of the places I'd seen on my trip so far. She was very taken with my journey, and when I asked if she'd ever consider travelling herself, she answered with an emphatic, "No, never!"

Finally she grasped both my arms in her hands and shaking her head solemnly with some tears in her eyes, she said, "I can't believe you came to me. I can't believe you came here. What an evening we've had!" That truly did astound and touch me deeply. I must say, I did feel that we had shared some real warmth between us, and taken great ease in each other's company over that cup of tea.

On my way up to my room I stopped at the bathroom, and when I pulled the chain afterwards it set off such a racket in the depths of the house that it sounded like a great beast had awoken in the basement. I made a note not to have another cup of tea and need to use that bathroom in the night.

Wednesday 27 May
Torrin to Dunvegan, Skye

The other guests turned out to be a middle-aged English couple whom I met the next morning when they joined me at the table for breakfast in the dining room. Around the walls of this room were all the family portraits, from the black and white wedding picture of Mr and Mrs A, through to two beaming round-faced girls who I took to be the granddaughters. Our cheerful hostess served us efficiently with a hearty Scottish breakfast brought through from the kitchen I had sat in with her the previous night. The other couple talked quietly together and I finished my meal and prepared to use the bathroom one final time before departing. Going in to the bathroom and cleaning my teeth I could hear through the wall the soft sound of cutlery clinking and their conversation quite clearly: I would NOT awake the monster in the deep again. I brought the bed linens down for a grateful Mrs A, who must surely be tiring of making beds, breakfast and washing linen, but she assured me again how much she enjoyed running the B&B. At nearly 80, I felt it a shame she did not have someone to do this side of the work for her. When she only requested £25 for the night, I tried to give her more, but she refused and found me some change. The best I can offer her is a testimonial in this story as to what a wonderful experience I had in her care that one night in Torrin. By the way, I learned as I was going that the water we looked out on is Loch Slapin – the name of the B&B now made perfect sense.

It was raining when I stepped outside to my car, and turned in the direction of Broadford again. I was growing quite good at discerning the subtlety in different grades of grey having seen so much of it. The clouds a varied range of warm grey, the mountains steel grey going down to yellow grey, and the lochs more of a black or purple grey. I'm sure that had the weather been balmy for most of my trip I could not have enjoyed it more than I did through the

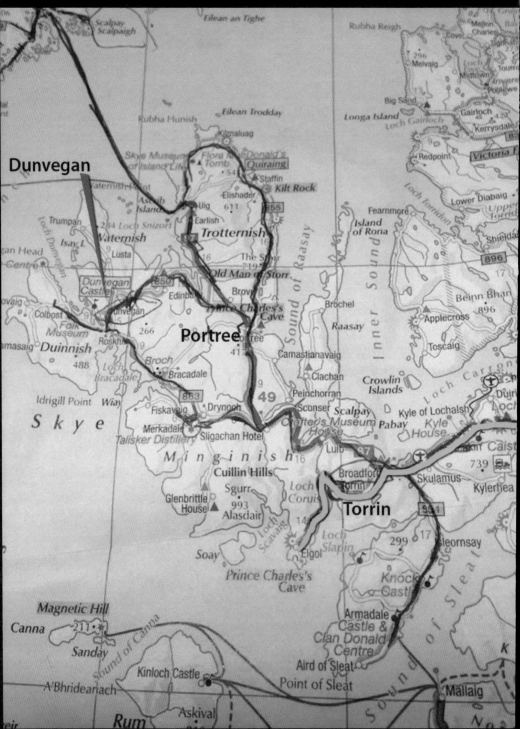

rain, wind and clouds for the month I was there. I drove straight through Broadford, there being no café open yet, and turned towards Portree on route 87.

I had forgotten the sheer glory of that range of mountains into which the road turns after Luib. Suddenly you find yourself coasting down a horse-shoe shape with the loch in the centre between peaks so old they've become rounded at the top and each one a weighty presence leaning over the road. Far on the other side I could see the road going up similar mountains to disappear around the corner. At the apex of the horseshoe and the lowest part of the road, is a gushing waterfall, and fortunately, a shoulder on the road for cars to pull in and take photos. Naturally, I did.

It is 26 miles or 42 kms to Portree from Broadford, and I was there in good time to stop for coffee and a cake in The Granary Coffee shop in the main square. I had eaten here before on the minibus tour a few years earlier and was pleased to see the place was still bustling. Afterwards I stopped at the Tourist Information Centre and booked in some accommodation at Portree on the night I would return from Harris and Lewis. Portree is a lively town, with a bustling central square taken up with car parks and bus bays. It actually IS a square, (not the triangle often so named a square in other places), and all around the edges are shops, hotels or restaurants in shades of black, grey or white.

Much as I could have spent the rest of the day here, I wanted to explore as much of the island as I could. And so I drove up through rain to Uig, where the ferry would leave for Harris on Friday, and then rounded the peninsula and came down through the Quirang, an amazing rock formation which is popular among hikers. The countryside all around the cliff edges of this peninsula is sloping grassland and pasture, rich green at this time of year. Stone fences and white crofts abound, and the wind slices up the slopes without trees to act as windbreak. I was driving along enjoying the windswept hills and rock formations when another historic village caught my eye. I parked and paid the entrance fee willingly, and clutching my coat tightly around my neck, wandered around these crofts full of farm equipment and photos, and reconstructed croft kitchen and inset box beds. Set as they were in the windy exposed sides of the hill, I could only imagine how bleak it was to live there.

Further south is the famous 'Kilt Rock' formation, a cliff face so multi-toned that it resembles a tartan, and these cliffs are sheer walls down into the sea. Added to that glorious sight is the long white waterfall next to the viewing platform, and it is almost impossible not to get a good photo. It tested me today though, being incredibly windy and wet, but I managed to shoot an almost sideways picture of my face against a blur of distant cliff and fall.

I also found the 'Old Man of Storr' – a jagged pinnacle of rock that rises high against the skyline. It is part of the Trotternish ridge and once the 'Old Man' had an 'Old Woman' with him, but she has since collapsed. This area was a popular hiking place, even in this weather, for the road nearby was full of vehicles. I took what photos I could in the rain, and continued my journey south to return to Portree.

Finding 'The Granary' so full that people were being turned away at the door, I went next door to a bustling bakery and purchased something like a bannock to 'tide me over'. I took the road towards Dunvegan and the B&B where I would be staying tonight, but my intention was to go out on the Duinnish peninsula and look around first. This area had its hills and some low mountains, but was farming country, green and a bit swampy in places because of the recent rain. Of course, everywhere there were sheep, and many had the distinct black faces and horns of the local breed in the Highlands. I was growing more accustomed to driving on the one-lane roads, avoiding pot holes, sheep, oncoming traffic and cliff edges. I never really got used to the road signs that preceded bridges or narrow corners, which said, 'Oncoming traffic in middle of road'. There were a few close calls – that's all I'm saying.

Kilt Rock

Old Man of Storr

Dunvegan Mountains

At Dunvegan I stopped at the first cafe I found. This was – comparatively – a busy town – situated on the edge of Loch Dunvegan, a part of the sea that stretches a good way inland. (I've discovered that 'Loch' means 'Lake' but it also seems to mean 'Cove' as well.) There was a cluster of about five shops including the cafe overlooking the bay, and a few roads of houses leading down to more shops further down. I don't want you to get the impression by 'town' I meant something bustling and built up. This first cafe had a splendid window filling up a wall and offering a wide view of the dark water and the land on the far side, and beyond that some dark shapes that rose up into the low clouds. There was a fishing boat loading up directly below, about to head out into the squally water. I asked the waiter when he approached whether there were mountains in the distant view, and he said just a couple of flat-topped ones, and indicated a painting on the nearest wall. It felt very good to be perched on a chair facing out into the squally conditions overlooking the sea, chomping on cake and sipping coffee. Reluctantly I departed the warmth of the café and slid behind the wheel of my little car again, heading out on the Duinnish peninsula, which was the land in view on the other side of the Loch.

The further out I went, the rougher the road became, and the more frequent the passing bays. I glimpsed a sign on a driveway? road? as I drove past entitled 'Uiginish Farmhouse B&B' and knew I'd found my turn off for the night. It being only early afternoon I continued toward Colbost, regularly pulling aside or passing other people in waiting bays. I was gliding through gently undulating land, dotted with white cottages, and the sky had cleared enough to show as rich blue with scudding white clouds chasing across it. When I reached a fork in the road at which a tiny whitewashed 'General Stores' sat, its two windows and door covered in notices and a red postbox in front, I knew I must be at Colbost. There were one or two other buildings nearby, but no other indication of a town. The road continued past, up, down and around through tufted meadows of cottages, sheep and many derelict crofts. Occasionally, and astonishingly, I sometimes had to pull over for a cumbersome campervan or bus, all negotiating this backwater with me. For all the narrowness of the roads, and the amount of traffic on them, I never saw a dead sheep in all my travels!

Continuing on the B884 I drove up a hill and past a building that had the words 'Skye Silver' on its placard. It was one of those instances where you are well beyond the point at which you saw the sign, and still reading it in your mind, and I realised belatedly, it was a silversmith's workshop. [Mental note to return later.]

I followed the coastline, and ended up on a tiny metal road that veered around a corner to end up near some tractor and work vehicles, and what looked like mesh nets out in the water. Just at the point the road had turned toward the sea, I glanced across the mouth of the Loch to a far distant coastline with steep cliff faces, and saw what must be a tremendous waterfall plunging over the edge and down.

Retracing my drive along the road and turning off at a side road, I reached Glendale, distinguishable only by a set of houses in close proximity, where I crossed a river and started to make my way up the other side. It was bewilderingly difficult to know which way to turn when the little road split and was feeling more and more like it would peter out at some point soon. I got to a place on the map called Milovaig, and turned up a side road finding myself driving through a muddy farmyard replete with old equipment and tractors and a bull. Somewhere off in the distance a dog barked, and I pulled into a path leading on to a farm track and turned the car. For all I knew it was still the main road to Upper Milovaig, but

the deserted driveway feel of it had finally got to me. I returned past the belligerent stare of the bovine, over the bridge and back toward the township of Colbost. Don't think for a moment I was unhappy. I was driving a car in one of the most remote spots in the UK, a long way from home, surrounded by a palette of lovely ochre and purple colours, and an ever changing tapestry of

mountains, meadows, and water. I felt amazingly safe.

When I drew close to 'Skye Silver' I parked and walked in through the doors. It was indeed a shop selling silver items and jewellery. Two people chatted behind the counter, and I wandered around admiring the jewellery and totting up what I could afford in my head. Finally I chose a Celtic design of 'The Tree of Life' as a pendant, and they wrapped it and were very effusive and helpful.

I drove back to the signpost for the 'Uiginish Farmhouse'

and turned on to the track. It was a very long drive, winding up and around the fields, and through a flock of black-faced sheep some of which rested on the road. At times the potholes were so large, I swerved on to the grass to avoid them. I went past two other houses, neither of them my B&B before the road came to rest among the sheds and back buildings of a large cream farmhouse. I believe the road continued on beyond the buildings, but I had seen the sign and knew I had reached my destination.

The back wing of this farmhouse was entirely set up for bed and breakfast. A very efficient woman responded to my knock, and smilingly led me up to my room and ensuite on the first floor facing out over the back paddocks. It was all very neat and clean and my queen-sized bed looked plump and cosy. I rested for a while, feet up, and uploaded photos on to my blog with the wifi now working on my I-pad. Costing only £37 for the night, I was feeling very pleased with myself. Closer to dinnertime, I drove back to Dunvegan, avoiding the potholes and sheep. Tonight's dinner was at a little Italian Bistro overlooking the Loch at Dunvegan, eating a seafood chowder that was delicious, accompanied by a glass of sauvignon blanc, in an almost empty dining room.

Thursday 28 May
Dunvegan to Broadford, Skye

Looking out through my window into the back yard of the Uiginish Farmhouse, I saw just a skittering of white clouds on a deep blue sky.

Time to go and see Dunvegan Castle and touch base with the MacLeods!

Breakfast was downstairs in a bright modern dining room with gingham curtains and a range of separate tables, all clearly delineated for each room guest. Our hostess was all pleasant efficiency, and the whole experience was enjoyable if a little distant. (I was basing it on last night's stay and the warmth of that hour in the kitchen in the croft house.)

With my usual surge of pleasure at setting forth into a new – Scottish – day, I negotiated the pits and holes of the driveway, avoided the sheep sleeping here and there on it, and turned left toward the township again.

Continuing on north, through the township another mile or so, the castle car park appears on the right-hand side and the stately stone entrance itself on the left. Dunvegan Castle has the honour of being 'the oldest continuously inhabited castle in Scotland' and the clan chiefs have lived there for 800 years. I mean, I just HAD to go in now.

Crossing the bridge over to the elegant and well-maintained castle, I could see the sea just beyond and the ground below and around full of trees, walkways and gardens. When I was greeted inside the door, we were told there was no photography allowed and were given a nudge in the direction we should set forth on our exploration. I was also made aware in some of the notices around that this was where Flora MacDonald had spent her last years, and it was also a place that the 'Bonnie Prince' had spent time at.

Dunvegan Castle

The other intriguing thing about this castle were the glimpses of something 'fairy' in many items – the first one I passed being a set of stairs leading up into the next level, near the bed chamber occupied by the clan chief. This was barricaded off with a small notice nearby saying, 'Fairy Stairs'. (I believe there were some 'Fairy Falls' somewhere nearby but I never saw them). By the time I had made it through to the northern end of the castle, through rooms of MacLeod portraits and paraphernalia, I was in an area of the castle looking out toward the mouth of the sea. In this room were some items of special interest (to me). In a huge frame on one wall was the 'Fairy Flag', so named because it has been ascribed with magical properties. It is an extremely old, ripped and tattered piece of yellowish silk, about 46 cm square. Some have associated the flag with the Crusades, or even a raven banner used by Viking leaders. It has many mythical properties associated with it, and various warnings as well, and has been seen as good luck for the clan in times of need. I enjoyed staring at its ancient and threadbare fabric, thinking of its age and secrets and feeling a little thrill go through me.

Nearby are some other fascinating objects – the waistcoat that actually belonged to Bonnie Prince Charlie, and the painting of him wearing it, and in a lower glass cabinet, Flora MacDonald's corset and some of her personal items. (I shudder to think how she would actually feel about these things being picked over and displayed all these years later). Standing in the middle of the room was a huge claymore, heavy and menacing, and my memories of Culloden and the men struggling across that barren moor with weapons like this came surging back. From the window, I took the only photo I was allowed, out over the sea – imagining many people in previous years standing just where I was, looking out at the mouth of the Loch as it opened onto the ocean, waiting for news, returning ships or oncoming battle.

Outside again, I wandered around the grounds enjoying the

ponds, the bluebells and other spring growth in the gardens, before crossing the road to continue my journey.

I took the A863 south, through Roskhill and Bracadale in a rolling countryside high above the sea in places, and offering some splendid panoramic views. My paraphrase of a local saying: 'Four seasons in one hour' held true, and these photos show blue skies at on the far left and curtains of rain covering the land and sea on the right. The customary white washed dwellings and dark roofs dotted intermittently over the ground, which was still showing signs of the winter in straw-like patches among the green growth everywhere. Heather abounded here but was not the purple I expected, but more of a burgundy, and looked lovely with the yellowed grass and the steel-blue sea. As you can see, I was already arranging my palette for painting upon my return. The sheep looked much more like our own, and the setting so similar to pastoral scenes in the Waikato, that if I couldn't see those white-washed houses, I would have believed myself in the North Island of New Zealand.

And then we passed another ancient broch, a mound of carefully laid stones set against the skyline on the left. I did not get out into the wind and rain to climb the muddy steps leading up to it, having seen such splendid examples of these old burial places only a few days ago.

The inlet of sea (Loch Harport) that I was following on my right, finally tapered out at a point near Drynoch, and here a signpost pointed out the famous Talisker Distillery. Naturally, I drove in that direction up on the other side of Loch towards Carbost, the seaside port where the whisky was made. Talisker is the peaty whisky I had tried at my evening tasting with Angie and husband in Beauly, and although I enjoyed it, I preferred the less peaty Cragganmore whisky they had.

There was a bit of negotiating to do on the road getting down to the port, it being quite busy and the roads not up to the load of traffic using them. I was lucky and found a newly relinquished park opposite the big white buildings of the Distillery, set rather prettily against a stream that flows beneath and out to the sea. I joined the flow of human traffic in to the whisky shop and roamed the shelves interestedly. There was a lot of money being exchanged, and whisky being sampled, but when I saw I'd be parting with well over £50 – there being no smaller bottles for sale – I remembered my preference for the Cragganmore and just enjoyed the thick aromas. I also greatly enjoyed the sight of the 37-year-old bottle worth £2046.75 in a display stand, and tried to grasp what a dram of that would taste like, much of it evaporating off the tongue as it slipped down. (I apologise now, to any real whisky drinkers reading this story, appalled that I was there and walked away empty-handed.)

Quite apart from the Talisker Distillery, this is a very pretty little seaside town. Most of the buildings are white, with dark grey roofs, and set as they are against green countryside, distant mountains, and with the loch right at the doorstep, it is a pleasant place to stop. I took the car then on a meander out into the hills

along the coast, stopping to photograph the occasional empty and roofless old croft.

Back on the A863, I continued on until it joined the main road between Broadford and Portree. Of course, at this junction where the Sligachan Hotel has a large car park, I had to stop and get out to take in the impressive views all around. Adding to the natural splendour of this spot, the function about to take place in the Hotel was a wedding, and three brightly clad bridesmaids in pink were running across the road to the stone arched bridge to festoon it in rose petals, ready for the bride. The wind was whipping their dresses and hair all around, and only I and one or two others were there to appreciate the moment all those red petals descended briefly upon the rounded arch before they were swept up by the breeze and tossed away. Disgruntled, the girls returned with half-empty baskets, but I savoured the moment and tucked it away in a happy place in my mind.

From the road, and facing west, there is a scene that must be on all photographs taken by visitors to Skye: A wide babbling stream of dark water bouncing over rocks, a three-arched stone bridge spanning it, rough terrain in the foreground, and impressively high peaks spread wide in the backdrop, snow-covered in winter, but highly textured in green and brown today. Enthusiastic walkers in bright hi-vis gear were striding purposefully to or from the bridge, but my only foray into exercise was the effort to reach the part of the road that gave me the best angle for my photos.

Back I drove through the splendour of those mountains that preceded Luib, and I stopped once again at the waterfall in the central curve of the horse-shoe shaped road.

It was mid-afternoon when I drew in to Broadford again. (I was getting quite familiar with this stretch of road.) I had also noted on my first day through, that the place I would stay this third night on Skye – The Hebridean – was on the main road overlooking the water. It looked reasonable enough – just an ordinary three-storey building, with restaurant on ground floor and eight windows on each of the floors above. The car park was across the road, and I walked to the side door and knocked. After a while, I heard tread on the other side and then a rather angry face appeared at the door. He barely gave me time to say I was booked in for the night, before pointing to a notice nearby stating check-in at 4pm. I apologised as the door was shut against me.

Nothing daunted, I returned to the car and took the opportunity to go and see something of the little town I've stayed in twice in the past – Kyleakin, just to the left of the Skye bridge. Here I found the cosy bar next to Saucy Mary's Lodge, the backpackers that was so familiar to me, and settled in a cosy spot to have coffee and upload photos to my blog.

It was a safe 5pm when I returned to The Hebridean 'Hotel' and registered my stay with a now more temperate manager. He took me up one flight of stairs and along a dingy corridor to a small room bearing all the signs of frequent occupation and indifferent care. I was not too disturbed, because I had, after all, signed up for a wide breadth of experience on this trip, and this looked assuredly like it would be an experience. The floor squeaked under my tread as I made my way down the corridor to the bathroom that I'd share with another on this floor. I had a small basin in my room, and two thin towels slung over the chair. The single bed seemed clean, but could never be described as plush. A boiler type heater sat under the window, which looked out toward the sea. In the distance a door squealed open noisily, and above me, the distinct sound of running children pounded down from the room above. I ruminated briefly about the £40 this was costing as over against the £37 from the night before, but let it go.

I went downstairs to the restaurant for dinner, and found my moody host to be also the chef, which explained a lot. In writing up this account I cannot remember what I ate but I do remember enjoying seeing the family of four whose room was over mine, and

the two young girls whose lively action had bounced some plaster off my ceiling. The parents seemed particularly disgruntled and had the waitress return a couple of times to answer questions about the menu. The other tables filled slowly with a range of different groups, all most enjoyable to watch, from the four rowdy young men who had been at The Claymore when I went for dinner that time, to an older couple who barely said a word to each other. All in all, I was quite happy in my own company, feeling somewhat smugly, that at times it was preferable to be alone.

Afterwards I squeaked upstairs, swung the noisy hinges of the door open, and lay down for a while to watch the little television suspended in the corner. Soon after the sound of little feet upstairs alerted me to the return of the family of four, and I heard the splashing of water in a shower. In fact, the sound was so real and so present, that it took me a moment to realise it was seeping from ceiling to my open suitcase. I swung quickly off the bed and pulled it away, putting a rubbish bin in its place.

Down I went to find the manager, and instead found his wife, who returned with me to investigate the seepage. She apologised profusely, said she didn't want to disturb the family upstairs who already had issues with them over the lack of a door between their room and their daughters, and moved me to the room next door. It was all very exhilarating and not unlike 'Fawlty Towers'.

I pulled all my items to the room next door, including a spare pillow, and settled in to a room distinctly smelling of cigarette smoke. At least it was dry, and before long, I had drifted into an unbroken night's sleep, happy in the knowledge I was going to the Outer Hebrides tomorrow.

Friday 29 May
Broadford, Skye to Tarbert, Harris

The theme of the evening before ('Fawlty Towers') continued with breakfast at 'The Hebridean' this morning.

I discovered my allocated table downstairs, organised so that the chair back was toward the window and view – very in keeping with the type of service we were growing accustomed to. I didn't change it, feeling sure that the drama was going to be more lively facing inwardly. Soon the dining room was full of all the guests of the night before plus some who'd arrived after I left. My breakfast arrived in good time and was all I had come to expect: a lump of scrambled egg with a blob of thin smoked salmon quivering on top. (I don't know why I had hoped for a portion of hot smoked salmon fillet, but I had.)

We all sat chewing slowly to the morbid and troubling news bellowing out from breakfast television just around the corner. Every item of misery and murder was broadcasted to our silently listening room, as I swallowed down my salmon; from the woman viewing her dead brother's face now transplanted on a stranger, to some deep psychiatric issues in known psychopaths. The commentary continued as I ate my marmalade on toast. It seemed a fitting end to my stay, and I did have to stifle my giggles as I drained my coffee cup to its, yes, there were dregs.

Having driven over much of Skye already, I had only to go up through Portree to reach the ferry port at Uig today, so I decided to revisit some of the places along that spectacular coastline along the Sound of Raasay (where Kilt Rock and 'Old Man of Storr' were). The sun was out, the wind had died, and there was every hope of some better photos than the ones I had taken previously in the rain. I could journey up the east side of that peninsula, and then go over and down to approach Uig from the North. My ferry was to leave at midday.

Leaving Broadford, I felt the usual wonder upon seeing those ancient mountains when rounding the corner after Luib. They never fail to impress with their size and sheer weight of presence, and it is worth it to stop in that bay near the bottom of the curve in the road to just get out and enjoy the view again.

Reaching Portree and the now familiar square, I parked and went in to The Granary for a morning coffee.

With my buoyant state of mind restored and feeling refreshed, I drove up the coast to look at the 'Old Man of Storr' and 'Kilt Rock' with the sky mostly blue overhead and just light cloud. How different the same road felt approaching it in this state, than when I had last been here. There, sharply delineated against the blue, was the 'Old Man', and the cliff faces nearby had clear strata layers and were silhouetted against the sky.

The whole coastline up here is spectacular. The houses are the usual country homes: small, white with dark roofs, and often stone walls to keep the livestock in. The view out to sea shows a huge mountainous land in the far distance, with a very changeable ocean stretching between. The land is grassy for the most part, but occasional patches of heather amongst the rocky outcrops, and inland, those amazing projections of rocks and cliffs.

When I reached the car park of 'Kilt Rock' I was pleased that it was still fine, if blustery, and my photos reflect a very different day than earlier, with more clarity in the patterns of the 'kilt' strata layers, and brighter colours in grass and sea. I was very glad I had returned to have another look.

Going north from this point, the road becomes a single-lane with passing bays, long sloping fields of green grass, and that glorious ocean view most of the way. My one regret when I consider this day's drive is that I failed to notice Flora MacDonald's grave, which is near the top of this peninsula. I rounded the top and came down the west side until I was negotiating the steep curved road down into Uig port and the ferry building. It had cost my car and me £72.20 for a return trip on the ferry from Uig to Tarbert, and I had the documentation with me, but needed to go in and get the ticket, so I joined the lane marked for car traffic onto the ferry, parked, and went in to the building. A ticket collector walking up and down these rows of parked vehicles clipped my tickets and once he had passed, I left to find lunch at a café nearby.

There are a few places surrounding the ferry dock that offer refreshments. I walked around them all, from the bar nearest the sea, past the cottage offering soup and teashop items, and finally settled on a cheaper place right next to the ticket office. Settling on a choice of scone and coffee, I asked the person behind the counter to heat the scone and was told, "they don't do that". Nonplussed, I handed my money over and went to await my food. (How hard is it to put a scone in the microwave for a few seconds?) When it was finally deposited on my table with the coffee, it was cold, crumbly and hard, and attempting to apply the hard lump of butter to it, crumbled it even further. There was no jam. I returned it to the counter, saying it was stale and inedible. The replacement was brought with mumbled apologies and a comment that it was 'fresh'. It was only one day old hard, not two days, so I ate what I could of it. My suggestion: Avoid scones at the café beside the ticket office at the Uig dock. In fact, avoid the café altogether.

I watched the Calmac ferry arrive and turn, and soon enough, what seemed a huge number of cars, campervans, trucks and even buses, had driven on board and we passengers were finding seats in the comfortable cabin area above. This was the first of what would be six ferry crossings for me, and I had nervously read up about seasickness the night before. (Memories of crossing to Dublin many years prior still awakened some horror in me.) To my great relief, the sea was calm and the weather remained fine, if blustery, and in accordance with what I'd learned, I went straight out on the stern deck and sat staring at the horizon line. Before long I had forgotten why I was there for I was so enjoying being huddled in my scarf and coat, hood up, watching Skye recede before my eyes. It was amazing to know I was now heading to an even more remote place than Skye, and the furthest I had ever been from New Zealand.

The ocean was a deep dark blue, and way off on the distant horizon line the grey mountainous shape of the islands of the Hebrides became more defined. I felt very eager and full of anticipation for what lay ahead. When a sudden squall whipped spatters of rain against my coat, it took me a while to realise I was virtually alone on that side of the ferry, and I felt rather stupid when I joined the majority who were in the shelter on the other

side, looking much warmer. After an hour and a half, the distant outline of Harris and Lewis was sharp and focussed and I watched as we approached what looked like an island of round granite rock dotted with fragments of green grass in its clefts and hollows. The closer we drew to this rocky shore, I saw with greater definition the occasional white house alone on that hard surface, no trees to speak of, and a textured surface of heather and grass in the hollows. It resembled nothing less than the coat of an old animal whose main body lay beneath the sea.

As we drew near to Tarbert, we wove through a network of little rounded islands. The town appeared to be a cluster of larger two-storey buildings and dwellings in muted shades with some soft round trees throughout, and all these pressed closely in around the wharf and quay area. It all looked very inviting.

Once the front of the ferry was lowered on to the sloping ramp, I drove up and found a parking space where I could attempt to discover the whereabouts of my B&B for the night. The central streets were all close and – in some cases – one way, and behind the town a great round mound of granite rose up forming a backdrop. This was an old worn landscape, a place that had borne the ravages of time and weather. My address was as undefined as the ones on Skye, and in Gaelic: 'Tigh na Mara' in East Tarbert. I

called the number and the pleasant woman who answered gave me some brief verbal directions, and within a short time I had found the sign, and the driveway down to the house. A robust matronly woman in an apron met me outside and led me first through the  warm conservatory, and then up the stairs to my bedroom which sported a double bed and a single, as well as its own bathroom. It was all very clean and cosy, complete with lacy pillow shams and quilted tissue holder. And, according to the Lonely Planet Guide, which I was using to find my accommodation these days, the owner of this B&B was a keen baker and would provide cake with my tea. I was not disappointed: There on the tray with the tea things was a slice of fresh sponge cake. She told me there were two sportive young men coming, who  would be given the other two smaller room and share a bathroom, but as I was the only lady, I'd have the ensuite – and all this for only £30. Naturally, I was delighted. Soon enough another car parked outside with kayaks on the roof and the laughter and ribald conversation which accompanied the arrival of a couple of English adventurers.

From my bed I could look out through the window and see the departing ferry, weaving its majestic way through the little islands to return to Skye. I was truly well out of reach of my home in the outer most parts of the world.

Unpacked and washed I ventured out by foot to find a place for dinner, walking the five minutes or so back to the ferry area where I had seen a hotel and restaurant earlier. On my way down the hill I had called in at the post office, which was still open, and bought postcards and a CD of Skippinish 'Western Shores', thinking I'd take it home and play it when I needed a reminder of my trip. (It took me all of 24 hours to realise my car had a CD player in it which I could use.)

The bistro was very busy with backpackers, day-trippers, and tourists all recently disgorged from the ferry and looking for a meal, but they appeared used to the fluctuating crowds and no one was turned away. Soon enough I was perched in a cosy seat at a table, nursing a cider and uploading pictures to my blog.

The meal that night was the best sirloin steak I've eaten in a long while, and with rosy cheeks and probably a wobble in my gait, I made my way back up the hill to my room at Tigh na Mara. I sat for a long while on my bed staring out at the bright view outside (it did not get dark until after 10pm), taking in the harbour and the surrounding countryside, and watching a rainbow form and arch brilliantly over the now placid sea.

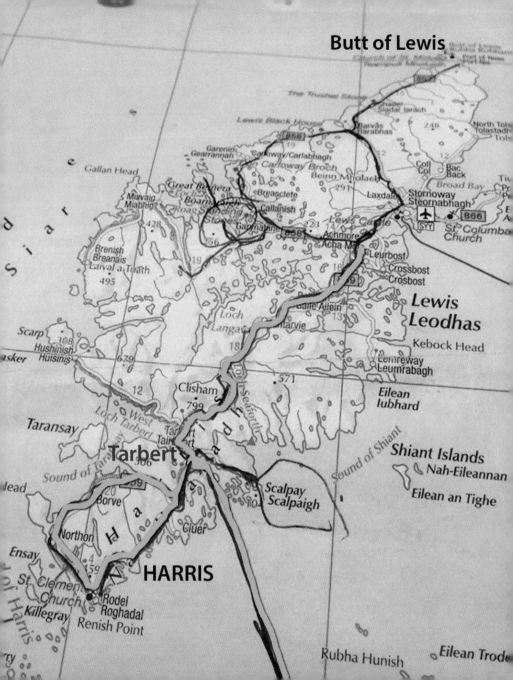

Saturday 30 May
Tarbert to Breascleit, Lewis

This was to be one of the most special days in my trip. As always, you have no idea when those days will occur, and that morning, sitting downstairs in the bright dining room overlooking the bay, I ate my cooked breakfast thinking about the direction I would head and how long it might take me. The two kayaking males on the other table barely acknowledged me initially, so caught up were they in their own plans for the day. Soon, though, courtesy obliged them to include me and they asked where I had come from and we talked briefly of our reasons for being there in Harris. I packed up my car and handed the gregarious host my £30 for the night.

My chosen route was south of Tarbert following the coast down into some of the most unique landscape I've ever driven a car over. Immediately I was in craggy rock country, on a narrow road – called 'The Golden Road' – that I sometimes saw rising in a shaky line up hills into the distance. For much of the time I was alone on it. This was a moonscape of treeless [14]granite mounds, covered lightly with tufty heather or grass, with occasional power lines weaving across the hills or following the road. Pools of dark water gathered in the deeper places, and occasional white crofts appeared nestled alone against the slope of a hill. Rounding a corner I might drive past some fat white sheep with black faces curled for warmth beside the road, or a lone red telephone box, and one time, suddenly, I passed a group of plastered buildings with a sign announcing 'Harris Tweed' on the gate. Naturally, I stopped and backed up. In this bare terrain, walking from the empty car park with my coat tucked around me against the chill, it was an equal surprise to open the door of the shop, and find it full

---

14. I have been calling this rock granite, merely for ease and because it resembles such, but in fact it is 'Lewisian gneisses, laid down in the Precambrian period, interspersed with igneous intrusions' McKirdy, Alan Gordon, John & Crofts, Roger (2007) Land of Mountain and Flood: The Geology and Landforms of Scotland. Page 94

of warmth, wonderful tweed and tartan everywhere, and a young saleswoman folding things behind the counter. If I blinked I might have believed I'd just stepped off the Royal Mile in Edinburgh. I compensated for my shock by a torrent of delighted chatter, which received moderate response from the young saleswoman, (who possibly didn't understand a word of it.) With a bag full of Harris Tweed items, I returned through the door back outside, into that completely 'other' world, and leaned into the wind to reach my car.

Sitting here in my office, in the heart of Auckland, surrounded by the noises of humans in close proximity, what I wouldn't give to be meandering up and down that landscape in Harris on the outer side of anywhere! I have the incredible texture of the place burnt into my memory, and the narrow, but rich, palette of greys, rust, maroon, ochre and blue.

There on Harris I would pull over to the side of the road often, alone in this strange setting, and feel as if I was in the space between worlds. One of my favourite photos of this area is one of a rocky hill, with patches of green grass and white daisies, a signpost and a distant wind turbine are silhouetted against the roiling sky, and two park benches are positioned at different places on the rock facing opposite directions. Who sits in these seats?

South I drove, past little lochs in hollows formed by grey rock covered in purple heather. They mirrored the sky and looked like they were made of mercury. All the signposts were in a mingled Norse/Gaelic, with interesting sounding names like 'Fleoideabhagh' or 'Aird Mhighe,' and on one occasion I saw a sign 'Skoon art café' and turned off the tiny road to rattle along an even tinier one.

It still astounds me that tucked away in this remote place I could come across shops or galleries that would be more likely in built up areas or cities. Skoon Café advertised on its placard 'quality espresso latte cappucino' along with traditional Scottish music and cakes. Perfect! Inside this – surprise! – white croft-type building with grey roof, is a cosy space with oil paintings by the resident artist, *Andrew John Craig, on the walls.

*www.skoon.com

Naturally, I availed myself of the opportunity to have some of that quality espresso and a bakery item, along with a browse around the studio. How I would love to paint in just this area, in just this sort of house, with just this kind of café. I trudged out to my car and set off on the 'golden road' again.

At Roghadal the road turns toward the west, and the stretch of sea at this lowest point on Harris is 'The Sound of Harris', separating Harris from North Uist. I only wish I'd had time to take the little ferry that negotiates the sandbanks and islands to reach that other island.

After a quick drive down and around the old church at Rodel, 'the only medieval building of any size to survive in the Western Isles', I continued on towards the west coast of Harris and the famous golden sand beaches I had read about.

When I reached Northton – in the lower west corner of Harris – it was to be further amazed. The salt flats here have created the most unusual jigsaw of round green islands, which today were a brilliant emerald green on the silvery blue water. On the far side a row of houses in different colours formed a line along the foothills, but the expanse between was like something out of The Hobbit. This whole area on Harris is full of bird life of all sorts, and has been occupied by man for over 5000 years, (if you can get your head around that!)

Sure enough, as I continued north along the rugged coastline, the beaches were visible as azure blue in colour flowing on to white sands. It is very rocky going down from the road, and a clear delineation of grey rock sometimes stained black with barnacles, divides the golden beaches from the land sloping down to them.

Remembering one of my bullet points for the bucket list, I made my way down the grassy slope, over the rocks and on to the course sand where I took off shoes and waded in to the frigid water. It is no wonder no one was frolicking in the surf! The water is absolutely clear, and from a distance is turquoise with whitecaps – absolutely gorgeous. Leaning over the fence taking shots, a little horned lamb with black face and socks looked up curiously at me, and when I baaa-ed at him, he moved in for a closer look. With the blue stripe painted around his torso by the farmer, and his striking colouring, he was the most designer lamb I've ever seen.

I drove slowly up this side of Harris, soaking up the glorious views and parking to take them in often. On the inward side I'd passed a golf course (apparently open since 1939) and imagine it has one of the best views of any course in the world. It would also have plenty of challenges, due to the constant prevailing wind from the sea. At some point today I had seen the CD player in the car and quickly installed my Skipinnish  music, appropriately named 'Western Ocean', and the music had been belting out loudly on replay ever since.

Reluctantly I left the sea behind and climbed steadily up on the A859 to cross the island and head back up to Tarbert. To my left some quite high peaks filled the skyline, and the land on the right fell away in gradual grassy slopes. Halfway up this hill I had a moment to register two men cutting peat in a deep trough beside a small

lake, and was past before I could stop in time. Naturally I braked and reversed back to park beside the road. They glanced at me as I  approached across the marshy ground and said something to each other, probably something about another nosy tourist. Standing on a bank nearby we shouted to each other to be heard. It went something like:

"Hello! I'm from New Zealand and I've never seen peat being cut. Do you mind if I take your photo?"

"No, that's fine. Are you on holiday then?"

"Yes, here for six weeks. This is my first day on Harris."

"What are your Scottish roots then? Do you have a clan?" (This question always comes up pretty early on).

"Yes, I have Urquhart in my background."

"Urquhart? (said the proper Gaelic way)" A pause, "Oh aye, not from around here then."

"No, and I've half English blood as well. I'm at war within myself, for there are London bobbies in my past as well and my Dad was a policeman."

The younger man nudged his father at his point, and said, "Dad is a retired Glaswegian policeman!"

"Aye, I've retired over here." They both showed more animation at this shared occupation than the clan information.

We said a few words more, and I got back in my car, ridiculously happy at the whole encounter.

Soon enough I was driving on the two-lane road into Tarbert again, but this time I continued through the town, and on up into the mountains that are the northern reaches of Harris. These are rounded mountains covered in heather, with black lochs at their base. The sky was heavy with clouds that brushed the top of the peaks and roiled above me in constant movement. The largest of the bodies of water below the road was Loch Shiphoirt (Seaforth), being one of the lochs that formed the border between Lewis and Harris. It was a long drive up through this mountainous region to reach what I think of as the plains of Lewis. (It's not strictly true for some mountains are on the Lewis side, but my memories put Lewis as having more marsh and flat land.) Staying on the A859, I reached the port of Stornaway by early afternoon, and drove down into what was a bustling harbour and town centre. Parking in the central car park (pay and display of course) I set off to explore the lively little town, and eventually ended up at the library which also had a café. This called for another coffee and cake scenario, and a dabble with my device while I uploaded post and photos to the blog. I made a mental note to return here tomorrow (forgetting that it was Saturday and the library not open on a Sunday!)

Rested and ready to move on, my little black VW Polo nosed south out of Stornaway on the same road I'd arrived on, but 15 minutes south there is a petrol station and here the A858 heads directly west. I was still on a two-lane road and able to travel quite fast across this gently undulating land, mostly treeless and covered in grass or reeds, dotted with cattle and many lakes.

In the far south a lovely edging of mountains in overlapping shades of mauve and blue.

I had passed only a couple of small towns straddling the road, modest houses and a church or two, when I needed to shade my eyes from the lowering sun. There, silhouetted on a hillside, was something that looked like crooked teeth sticking up. A wave of excitement: I had found the famed Calanais (Callanish) Stones! After so long anticipating walking among these Neolithic marvels, to be driving up to them through some scattered housing and little suburban roads was amazing. I parked and made my way up to the visitors centre, offering my Scottish Explorer Pass, confident that at last it would prove worthwhile having one, and was told I could go to the stones without it. (It did mean I could go and watch a little movie in the next room for free though.) Not wanting to waste any more time, I tightened my scarf, did up my coat and headed out into the wind, following a well worn track around some grassy mounds. There, through a gate and stone wall, these remarkable stones. Five or six people wandered as I did, taking photos, staring in some wonder at these flat light grey stones, jutting out of the ground and coming second only to Stonehenge in significance. The innermost circle of these are dated from 2900BC and there are 33 of these monoliths standing in a Celtic cross shape. I set up my I-pad on self-timer and, for the blog, took one or two of me touching the stones, as Claire did in Outlander. There has been much written about the significance and meaning behind these Callanish stones, everything from solar alignments, to lunar movements, and I'll leave you, the reader, to search those out. Suffice it to say, I'd love to have returned at different times of the day and season, for I'm sure they look quite different depending upon light and mood. Just to place my hand on a surface that was touched by another human hand nearly 5000 years ago sent some shivers down my spine all the way to my toes.

I exhausted my scope of things to do and thoughts to have, and started back to the car, enjoying the sight of a bewildered flock of sheep, all wondering what the constant fuss at the top of the toothy hill was.

Only a short distance further along the road I drove in to a small settlement called Breascleit, and at the first road turning off at the right was a sign saying 'Loch Roag Guest House'. (Once again, the address was simply: 21 Breascleit, Lewis.) There were a few B&B's up this road, all two-storey relatively modern buildings, and the owner of mine came out to greet me, saying he'd put me in the other of his houses instead. I reparked in the driveway of the house below, and registered with this red-cheeked and jovial man, who led me upstairs to a corner room with windows out towards the loch. He showed me the dining room downstairs that took up the whole of the front of the house with windows over that splendid vista, and said that they were serving pork loin for dinner and homemade cheesecake if I cared to stay. Of course I was interested!

The pre-dinner time was spent flat on my back on the single bed, relaxing after all the driving this day. I was able to make a cup of tea and refresh myself in my own little bathroom attached, and thought the £50 – if more expensive than the night before – well spent. I had a thoroughly enjoyable meal (£25) cooked by my host's son, who was a capable chef, and had a conversation with a couple from the next table. They had been Glaswegians before moving to England and felt the urge to go and do the Hebrides at last.

It being so light outside, I went down the road for a walk after eating, past fields hopping with rabbits, and small groups of sheep behind the fences further down. Everywhere the ground was marshy and puddled with water. Across the main road is the husk of what used to be the post office, merely concrete walls now, but sporting a tiny fireplace and chimney in what must have been the smallest PO in the UK.

I picked up couple of stones from the bank leading down into the waters of the loch, and turning made my slow way back up the road and to bed.

Sunday 31 May
Breascleit, Lewis

Ah, the bliss of awakening to two realisations! 1: I was on the Isle of Lewis and Harris in the Outer Hebrides, and 2: I didn't have to pack and move on because I was staying two nights.

Just when I thought life could not get better, I went downstairs to breakfast and found out that nothing, and I mean NOTHING, is open on a Sunday – not a café, not a shop, not even a tourist attraction. Now this was something overseen in all my planning. However, my chatty host suggested I go to a Gaelic church, which WOULD be open, and enjoy hearing their acapella singing. He told me the service would be at noon in an indistinguishable hall on the other side of Breascleit.

I considered it all the way out the door and into the squally conditions outside. I ruminated on it as I turned onto the road north and adjusted the wipers. Maybe I just would make it back by noon.

The next hour and a half was spent following a coastline just out of sight on my left, along a two-lane road, through little townships of fairly unremarkable houses. It would probably have made more of an impression on me if it had some of my favourite things in it: a view of the sea, trees, mountains, lakes.

As it was, it was distinguishable by one very impressive factor: it was mostly a huge swampy plain. The initial road I drove along had been zigzagging with some pretty little coves, and green grass dotted with rocks on the banks. At one point I pulled over to investigate a signpost to some standing stones, but could see through the marshy field they were quite small and did not go further.

At Carloway (Carlabhagh) there is a huge broch called Dun Carloway, notably the 'most complete and spectacular in the Western Isles'. Knowing it was closed, I merely observed it as I drove past, a huge conical shape on the skyline.

Just beyond Carloway is a road pointing off to a restored blackhouse village at Gearrannan, comprising croft houses used right up until the mid-20th century. These feature double drystone walls, low roofs and thatch, made out of local materials. The houses in this village are available for rent by tourists.

Soon after Gearrannan, the road stays pretty straight for the rest of the long haul north to the Butt of Lewis. In keeping with the bland countryside, the weather had turned grey again, and I kept fighting the sensation I was in No Man's Land. The swampy plain to my right was sliced into at regular intervals for peat, and often I saw stacks of it drying in long rows beside the cutting. The houses were small and plain with few gardens, and there were no trees to speak of. Occasionally I passed an empty husk of an old croft house, still in the place it had stood for years, but only a skeleton of stone walls and collapsed roof now. I wondered then as I do now what the occupants did for a living – or for fun, for that matter, because I feel sure I would go slowly mad. When at last I reached a more built up settlement called The Port of Ness, the northernmost point of Lewis, it was almost a relief.

Of course, these are purely my impressions on a wet Sunday in this remote place, and I feel certain that, judging by my encounters with all the hardy highland people I have met, the life inside those houses and villages was warm, friendly and full of

music and enthusiastically kept traditions. And quite likely, those communities could teach my own techno-rich urban community at home something vastly more important to know about neighborliness. But I digress.

I had reached the sea and could go no further, which meant that the Butt of Lewis lighthouse must be nearby. It did not take long to find it, although with my nose pressed up to the streaming windscreen, and potholes gauged into the road surface, I thought it surprisingly badly kept for such a distinguished landmark. Visibility was limited, and so the sensation of standing at the end of the world did not overwhelm me as I had hoped. In fact, standing at all was difficult once I prised the door open and ran through puddles to the noticeboard. Clinging to my hood to stop it from flapping off, I held the camera with the other hand, and kissed the sign saying 'Butt of Lewis', just so I could say I had done it. The wind coming off the sea was tremendous, and there was no line where the sea met the sky, just a soft merging of pale grey into grey. I pressed myself into the squall to go and see the edge of the cliff and looked

down. A vibrant finger of turquoise water between jutting rocks dotted in green and – pink? – yes pink!

Hearing the sound of a huge vehicle making its way towards me, I sprinted for the car and was happy to pull out of the car park as the tour bus stopped to let its passengers off. . .even here, in this remote and bleak outpost.

It was 11am, and I had an hour to get back down to Breascleit if I wanted to attend a Gaelic service. There was no time to waste. Back down the same straight road I drove, until a few hills rose around me, and the sea came in to touch the road in places. Once again the sun had come out, Skipinnish was playing, and all was right with the world.

Just where he had said it would be, my host's little church was signposted at the end of town, and a neat row of cars sat in the huge car park. Apparently he went to the English service at 10am, so I was definitely on my own in this venture. I opened the outside door and was virtually blown in by the wind, and shutting it behind me turned to see three startled men's faces looking back frozen in the act of talking quietly together. One of them jerked into sudden animation, and coming forward extended his hand in welcome, smiling uncertainly. We introduced ourselves, and he said with some feeling, "You know this is the Gaelic service?" I said I did know that, and wanted to hear the singing and see what it was like. Nodding, he put down the Gaelic bible he was about to offer me, and reached for an English one, which I took before proceeding in to join the congregation. I can only imagine how they looked at each other as I went in and sat down in the second to last pew.

The first thing that struck me was that there were about twelve pews, divided by the aisle, to the front of the church, where a three tiered arrangement of podiums and lecterns denoted the presence of the minister and his presiding officers. From the podium there were nothing but empty pews all the way back to the last four rows at the back. I was seated just behind those last four pews, which were all tightly packed with waiting parishioners. My eyes flicked to what I could see of the minister, wondering whether I had unwittingly subjected myself to a Hellfire and Damnation sermon, albeit in a foreign tongue. From this distance he did look rather severe.

The second thing I immediately noticed was that all the females wore hats. These hats did not appear to be particularly stylish, or even the same shade of colour, or match the outfit in any way, but were perched jauntily on heads, or pinned roughly, in keeping with the old tenet that suggests a woman's head should be covered to denote submission to their husbands or the minister, before God. My own uncovered head, wisps of hair escaping the braid, was quite plainly in flagrant disregard to this custom. I was not too troubled (and neither were they, when I later chuckled about it after the service!)

The minister stood and addressed his distant parishioners in Gaelic, and to my joy, I heard some English words interspersed – a psalm number. Quickly turning to it in my own book as I stood with the congregation, I suddenly heard a strong male voice chant out from the front. It was an elderly man seated on the tier below the minister. At the end of the phrase he sang, everyone around me burst into song and continued this way for a few lines, and then fell silent while he sang again. This was the pattern each time they sang a psalm. The white-haired man way up the front chanted out the first line, and everyone else responded with the next few. Sometimes the song was quite long and, certainly, every tune was different. My fingers itched to open my I-pad and quietly video it all, but just when I reached to do so, the same man who'd welcomed me in to the church, eased himself onto a seat to sit directly behind me. Some unspoken rule of etiquette forestalled me from openly recording what was obviously personal and reverent. You will have to take my word for it, that it was lovely to hear.

After the singing, the minister stood and gave his sermon, and I could at least get a gist of what it was about by the simple fact that he had given the reference in English. As one who has sat in the pew many times in the past, it was of great interest to me to listen purely to intonation, and expression, rather than words. However even that palls after half an hour or so, and I was feeling quite droopy by the time we shuffled to our feet for the last songs.

We all went out into the bright blustery day, women holding on to their hats, and I found myself greeted and surrounded by friendly faces, shaking hands with many and feeling quite heartened by their warmth. The minister – who was not at all severe – introduced himself to me as Colum MacDonald, and I learnt a few things in our discussion. Regarding the singing, he told me that the singing leader knows about 50 tunes and chooses which one he'll use for each song he starts, and the congregation know how to respond to that tune. He asked me why I had not come to the English service (which he also gave the sermon at), and I told him I was interested in hearing the Gaelic spoken and the singing. After a short discussion about New Zealand and my travels, he invited me to join his family for lunch, although he himself would not be there long, as he had to go to take another service at 2pm elsewhere. I declined that generous invitation, and instead got back into my car and drove south to the island of Great Bernera, taking the turn off south of the Calanais Stones. I crossed a concrete bridge over to this little island (the first pre-stressed concrete bridge in Europe) and drove around the narrow roads enjoying the view of the sea and the rugged rocky landscape covered in little lochs. The name of the island is Norse in origin, as are many local names, deriving from extensive early settlement. At the furthest end of this island is a spectacular white beach, with blue waves and a strong wind prevailing, but additionally a car park and small graveyard. I got out of my car to read the notice and discovered I was standing at the site of the Bostadh Iron Age House. If possible, my excitement level notched up another level, and read with interest that as recently as 1996 archaeologists had unearthed a Norse settlement here of five Pictish houses. These dated back to just after 500AD. A reconstructed house was placed away from the site, just down the corner above the sands from where I was standing, and I eagerly set off in that direction. My imagination filled in the details, even as far as seeing the man of the house return across the waves and sand to approach the dwelling from the sea. With Norsemen firmly in my mind, I drove back over the bridge to the mainland and went further south into the area known as Uig, where the land is full of bumps and hollows, lochs, farms, and bays. I passed another red telephone box sitting out by itself on the road, a post box opposite. The hills were rising in the distance into mountains further out, and this was obviously the most dramatic that Lewis was going to get. I was coming here to see the golden beaches and azure waters, but mainly to see the place where the 12th century Viking chess pieces had been discovered, hidden by a raider in a hollow near the beach. At the southern end of Uig beach, yes, another spectacularly shining beach with azure waters, I found a road leading to a camping area,

and a statue standing visible for some distance, a beautifully carved wooden chess piece, commemorating the find of the ancient chess set. I took a selfie leaning on this king's lap, and feeling a tiny portion of my genetic makeup raise a fist in triumph to Valhalla. (There must be some reason for my strong bone structure, height, blonde hair, blue eyes, and love for sardines!) I felt it a pity that Stephen Hayward, the sculptor, had not seen fit to use my favourite Viking chess piece, the Berserker, for his model, which would have been more of a match with me, I'm sure.

Time for a break from driving, I parked down by the campervans and caravans and sipped some tea, still hot, from the thermos Fiona had given me in Edinburgh.

Driving back toward Stornaway, through a gorge of reddish rock and rushing brooks, then the flat countryside again, I sang along to Skipinnish and revelled in my freedom out here on the open

road in the Outer Hebrides. At Stornaway I parked outside a Hotel on the main road leading into the port, pleased to find it open, and spent the next hour having lunch and logging in to their wifi.

I was home at Breascleit by dinnertime after popping up the hill to see the Callanais Stones again on the way back (who could resist?) Despite the sounds in the kitchen and the smell of what proved to be a pork roast cooking, I took a can of lentil soup that had been rolling around on the floor of the car for a week, and asked if I could heat it. The chef's wife – daughter-in-law of the owner – smiling said she would sort it out for me, and upon returning five minutes later I was given a tray with my soup in a bowl and cutlery to take upstairs. I chomped happily on a piece of slightly stale French loaf and sipped my soup, hunched on bed watching television. Bliss.

Monday 1 June

Breascleit, Lewis to Portree, Skye

My ferry to Skye was leaving from Tarbert, Harris at 4pm this afternoon, and so I woke and breakfasted downstairs, keen to squeeze in all I could of the island before then. As a change from driving south on the A858 past the Callanish Stones, I decided to go up past Dun Carloway broch and find the only road (A857) that crossed that great peat marsh in the central part of Lewis, turning off just before Barabhas to go directly to Stornaway. This is only a half hour drive but would give me a great sense of the land that comprised the upper half of this island. (75% of the population of the Outer Hebrides live in Lewis alone, and most of them live in Stornaway.)

Approaching the Dun Carloway broch, with the blue sky overhead and the knowledge it was possibly open, I decided to go in and park. Unfortunately, it was not open until 11am, so I walked up the hilly path past a belligerent ram and his nearby flock, and went around the immense structure videoing my walk up to the door and regretting that I could not see inside it.

When I returned to my car, mindful of the warning to book a day or so ahead, I started a few phone calls to Loch Ness B&Bs for the night after next. I had made a a couple of enquiries and received as many rejections, and was just leaning back in the seat wondering what to do when a brown bird with white underside and a red chest landed on the fence in front of the car. It was my first Robin Redbreast sighting and – inexplicably - I felt a surge of hope! One more call and I had secured a room at Drumbuie Farm for the 2nd June.

I cannot remember much about that road across to Stornaway. It went on and on over flat ground, with ridges of exposed black ground where peat had been successively removed. The horizon ahead was nothing but a long line and the only life I saw was contained within the cars that were rushing from one side of the island to the other, for what was probably business rather than pleasure.

Frankly, it was a relief to wind in through suburban streets and return to the central car park of this bustling largest town. I crossed the road eagerly intent upon a decent espresso but when I entered the open doors of the Hotel I had eaten at the day before found the restaurant was not open. A friendly porter told me to try the Chinese Restaurant on the corner, and somewhat dubious, I walked down there. Opposite was the library café, but it was not open on a Monday. Having nowhere else to go, I went in and up to the counter of the Chinese Restaurant, past tables of others having everything from pots of tea to Sweet and Sour Pork. The coffee was okay, but the pleasure of sitting quietly and using the wifi amidst the clatter of chopsticks and coffee grinder made it all worthwhile.

Like every other day I had experienced so far, the weather had turned completely around in the space of an hour, and was now wet again. Heading off south on the main road between Stornaway and Tarbert, the A859, I enjoyed the increasing number of mountains and the wide vistas the road afforded of the seas and lochs below. My heart went out to the cyclists I passed – and there were a few – all laden down with panniers and wet weather gear, and slogging up these hills on roads busy with heavy traffic. Loving my bicycle at home, there is no way I would want to do the Outer Hebrides on two wheels. I can still remember my amazement at a café where a father was buying hot drinks for his family; two boys of about ten and twelve, and his wife. They were travelling by cycle around Skye, and the youngest boy had become ill, but after a day of resting, was ready to go off on the roads again. We are not talking about a level cycle path through pretty woods here, we are talking about narrow roads, trucks and cars sharing said road, and a never-ceasing wind with regular showers: Fun, fun, fun!

When I finally drove down into Tarbert with rain spattering my windscreen at 1pm I had a few hours to spare before the ferry would be boarded, and so drove out on a single-lane road that wound around the coast to the little island of Scalpay, set in the outermost mouth of Tarbert harbour. This meandering road brushed up close to houses along its route, crossed little bridges and had one or two hair pin bends, before crossing a lovely elegant white bridge that spanned the sea over to Scalpay (it replaced the ferry services in 1997). The lighthouse on this island was the first one in the Outer Hebrides.

I am so glad I had time to come out here. The road wound up past little white houses on grassy lawns following some sharp contours on land that rises up gently to 104 metres. Fairly soon,

Scalpay

Portree Harbour

though, I was amidst the main township of An Acairseid a Tuath (North Harbour.)

What caught my eye straight away was a neat little cluster of buildings overlooking the dock below, and a sign in front saying 'North Harbour Bistro.' Opening the door to go inside and out of the grey weather, a blast of warmth hit me, and I was hit with a heart-warming range of sensations from the muted golden lighting and tweedy curtains and tablecloths to the delicious aromas of home cooking. I went to the window and looked down, seeing the little dock had a few fishing boats tied up and people moving about preparing to go out. My lunch was the most delicious seafood chowder I've had in a long while, accompanied with fresh crusty brown bread. If only I had another week on the island, it certainly is an area well worth exploring.

Back along the wandering stone road I went to Tarbert and was soon on the ferry ready to go at 4pm. I felt quite a pang standing inside the ferry looking back out at the disappearing land, through rain-specked windows. When – if ever – would I be back to fill in all the gaps in my exploration of the Outer Hebrides?

It seemed to take much longer returning to Skye across the water – perhaps because I was inside in the warmth of the cabin, on plush seats facing the wake of the boat, and seeing nothing but grey outside. I perked myself up with the knowledge I was on my way to Skye again and had yet so much of my trip ahead of me.

It was 6pm when the ferry drew in to the dock at Uig and the great line of trucks, campervans, buses and cars slowly drove up the ramp and then parted through the streets of Uig to North or South. It seemed a miserable drive in grey light, the wipers going steadily, and a winding formation of vehicles all going to Portree along with me.

Tonight I was staying at a B&B in Portree, which I had booked through the Tourist Office before I left Skye for the Outer Hebrides. I have mixed feelings about using the tourist office for finding accommodation. Certainly, at holiday times especially, places like Skye fill up fast. But if access to the internet had been reliable on my phone, I would likely have found this place myself, and saved £5 and the proprietor would have been a little richer too (the amount they receive is reduced, the extra going to the Tourist Office.)

'An Airidh' was one of a number of large houses offering B&B accommodation on the main street leading out of town, and I found it easily and parked. It looked straight out on Portree Bay and I immediately perked up. Tonight was going to cost £55 and the older man who answered the door led me down the ground floor hallway to the first room facing the back of the house. It was perfectly comfortable and had a single bed and a separate bathroom (I fought the sensation of being tucked away in the spare space because I was only a single.) Now if I was put on a table in the back of the dining room tomorrow . . .

After settling in I drove back in to the square at the centre of town looking for dinner, and walked in the rain through jostling crowds all doing the same thing, to about four places, all quite packed with tourists and locals. After that fourth rejection I followed some backpackers in to a unprepossessing hotel and bar on a side street and found the dining area only moderately full. Honestly, I cannot for the life of me remember what I ate, but it was hearty plain food of some sort, and I did not linger afterwards but made it back to my viewless room and collapsed on my bed, replete.

Tuesday 2 June
Portree, Skye to Loch Ness

In the morning I was one of the first to arrive for breakfast, and was very pleased to see that my table was set before the window. Things were set out very efficiently, from a buffet of homemade muesli through to not just prunes, but a bowl of fresh strawberries, raspberries and boysenberries. Naturally, I had a lesser form of the Scottish breakfast as well, and afterwards had coffee in the lounge chairs overlooking the expansive harbour. It was no longer actually raining (why I bother mentioning the weather I don't know), but it could turn either way.

I was off to roam among the mountains today. Never would another day be so obviously mountain-themed like this: going from the huge giants that dwarf the road from Sligachan Hotel to Luib, then following the lochs from the Kyle of Lochalsh through to Loch Ness.

This was my happy place: setting off from Portree with petrol in my car, Skipinnish in my ear, and the Highlands in my heart. Sure enough, the flat marshy ground flowing with little streams south of Portree led into the mountains, and I stopped the car to try and capture by panorama, the landscape of heather, brooks and distant peaks. Nothing but actually standing there could do it justice. In fact, I was to stop and start this car almost every few miles on this day, feeling woefully inadequate in recording all I was seeing, but obliged to try. I cast a jaded eye at The Hebridean in Broadford as I drove past, and sooner than I wanted to be, was driving over that graceful arch of the Skye bridge, the rippling ocean far below. I did not stop at the Kyle of Lochalsh, but continued on until I saw the Eilean Donan castle approaching on the right. Parking by the community hall of the township this side of the castle, I had a great view of the Eilean Donan from a different angle, though the photo shows a moody backdrop of rain-drenched hills disappearing into

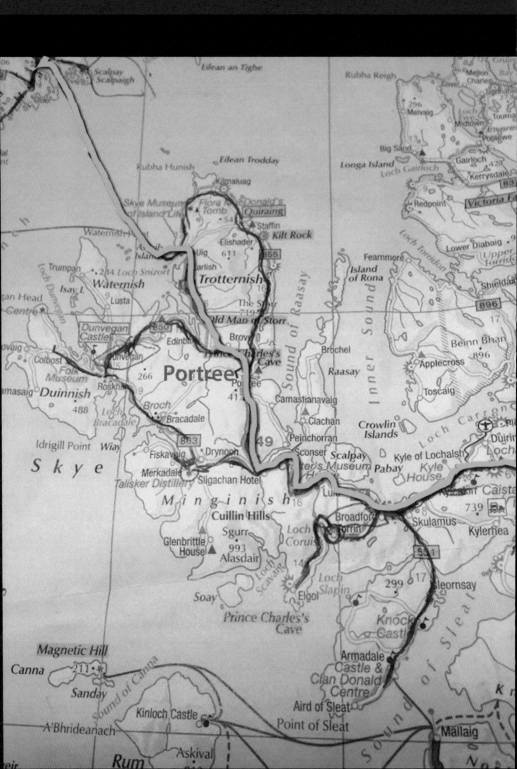

cloud. Time to walk across the gravel and in through the doors of a new coffee and bakeshop called 'All the Goodness' a few yards away. This had not been here two years earlier when the minibus I was travelling in had pulled in!

[15]A young couple runs 'All the Goodness', specialising in artisan coffee, and their own home-baked bakery items. As well as that, some lovely etchings grace the walls, and I bought one of a black-faced sheep against a mountainside, so reminiscent of my travels. The beaming young man at the counter wrapped it and said rather proudly, that his [16]wife was the artist. He called out to her, and she popped her head out of the kitchen so that I could respond to her personally. Even better! The coffee was wonderful and I took it and my fruitcake out to the car to look at Eilean Donan from there.

From the moment I arrived on the mainland, my car joined a stream of other vehicles coming and going on this busy road. I definitely felt 'out of step' with the majority of the traffic, coming so recently from the Outer Hebrides and the quieter pace of life there. As well, I was continually in awe of my surroundings and wanted to slow down and take them in, hence, the regular stops in passing bays along this stretch of road. I was not completely alone in this endeavour, for I found myself recognising the same cars again and again as we frequented the same layby points. This road – although busy – had not yet joined the A82 between Inverness and Fort William, which followed the bead of lochs from Loch Ness to Loch Linnhe. But the scenery on the A87 has its own glory. Back in Auckland, my sister has picked up the habit of saying, "Stop it!" when something becomes unbearably beautiful or cute. I found that little phrase on my tongue regularly as my car rounded curves in the road and I saw what lay ahead. In fact, "Stop it, Scotland!" should be my title for this adventure.

Every luscious curve of hill, glinting water sparkling in the lowlands, the craggy textured forms of countless peaks disappearing

---

15. www.allthegoodness.co.uk   16. Lorraine Tolmie www.lorrainetolmie.co.uk

and reappearing as cloud came and went, suddenly bathed in a surge of sunlight, then cast in shadow again. The uppermost parts of these mountains had of snow in their clefts and many were still white capped. You could have unfolded a camping chair and sat amongst the gorse and grass and stared for hours at the shifting scene in front of your eyes. All of my reading and movie watching involving kilted highlanders only served to increase my awe at their hardiness and tenacity, in traveling on foot through this landscape.

The road finally merged with the A82 at Invermoriston, right on the shores of Loch Ness. There is a large parking area here, near the ruins of an arched stone  bridge I had seen covered in snow in my previous trip. Then, it had all been sharp contrasts of black and white, and we had crunched our way over to look at the Highland 'coos'. Now those same cows (probably!) were munching steadily on grass and enjoying the attentions of a steady group of sightseers. I joined them. Holding my I-pad in one hand, set on self-timer, I backed against the fence and hoped the huge ginger horned head on the other side would not take the

opportunity to skewer me while I fiddled with my device. Up close, those horns are huge and lethal, and almost out of place on the fluffy big-eyed soft face beneath, looking benignly back at you.

There are a few lovely wooded walks leaving from this car park, and I retraced my steps of those years ago, which then had been in snow, but now were lively with bluebells and new grass. Our own bush at home in New Zealand is much wilder and denser than anything here in Scotland, so even these delicate paths winding through dappled shade and full of spring grasses and flowers were a novelty. I could not get enough of the profusion of bluebells and white daisies. Following the river back to the road, I passed the 'folly' – a stone summerhouse built over the rushing black waters – and reached the old bridge and my car again.

From Invermoriston, it is a fifteen-minute drive along the loch's edge to reach Fort Augustus, the southernmost point. The area was once called Killwhimin, but after the Jacobite Rising in 1715, it was renamed. General Wade built a fort here soon after, and it was captured by the Jacobites in 1745, just prior to Culloden. This is only part of its chequered history, but what I saw as I drove in, was the huge parking area full of tour buses and cars, jostling crowds of people on the streets, and a series of locks full of the

black water off Loch Ness and gently rising in height. I parked and paid, and joined the throngs walking toward the bridge and the Caledonian Canal.

The locks are impressive – starting at the level of Loch Ness itself, and in staggered steps rising two or three levels of locks to form the Caledonian Canal leading to Loch Lochy – the next body of water. These series of locks is repeated further south, which makes navigating between Inverness and Loch Linnhe on the western coast of Scotland, possible.

Fort Augustus is set up for the tourists, with plenty of restaurants, convenience stores, large public toilets, and various museums and gift shops. What took my eye though, was the advertising for a boat trip out on to Loch Ness.

Before long I was standing in a queue waiting to board one of a range of vessels offering trips on Loch Ness. We watched interestedly as a stalwart group of six young people donned heavy wet weather gear and belted themselves into seats on a jet boat. Moments later, it powered off down the narrow causeway into the open lake. About fifty of us climbed up into this more sedate two-level boat, and I secured a seat on the upper deck where I could spot Nessie if she rose to the surface and there I munched the sandwiches I had bought for lunch. When the boat made it out into the open water, I was relieved I had gone back for my coat and scarf. It was pretty cold skimming over the surface of that deepest of all lochs. There was a handy commentary over the loud speakers, alerting us to the presence of goats or deer on the nearby slopes – I caught a glimpse of a goat once – and giving a bit of historical information about the landslides that had happened and the fort when we passed it. All in all, it was a very pleasant hour spent looking out for Nessie and over too quickly by the time we turned and went back. Loch Ness is so large that our own hour-long trip barely encroached into the main body of the lake, and had I more days up my sleeve, I would have taken the longer trips

offered. Loch Ness is so large that it could hold all the water of the lakes in England and Wales combined.

At the little supermarket I restocked my car with the essentials: water, fruit, and perhaps a few bags of nibbles of some sort. My destination: Urquhart Castle and the place where a very distant clan ancestor was Sheriff for a while.

Half an hour's driving along the western shore of the loch, brought me to the car park and information centre. Back in 1989 when first I had come to see what I thought was the actual seat of my ancestors, there were just the castle ruins and a car park, and my friend and I had wandered around touching the stone walls and taking photos of the view from the tower across the loch. A painting I did of that view of the castle and lake behind it, still graces the living room of my mother's home. Now, it would be impossible to get that same unhindcred view because of the extensive landscaping and the walls that protect this ancient ruin. Not that it is a bad thing at all – the shop and information centre are well stocked and run, and there is a regular showing of a short film about the castle. A restaurant on site caters for the many visitors who now come to see this famous lake and castle, and many of the souvenirs are of course, of the elusive 'Nessie'. Two and a half years earlier, the minibus had passed by on my winter tour of the Highlands, stopping for a brief time on the side of the road for us to snatch photos of the distant castle through recently chopped bushes. Apparently the hedge we peeped through had been clipped to afford that 'illegal' view. We also performed a random and adulterated version of a haka back then, calling on Nessie to show her face.

With great satisfaction now though, I paid my £8.50 entrance fee (the Scottish Explorer Pass having expired!) and made the most of it. After lingering in the centre for a while, I walked out through the doors and on to the long path that goes down past a huge siege machine, before walking up the hill to the guardsman's entrance in the castle wall. There's a moat to cross first of course, and then the arch of the fortification itself, but I could not help being aware of how well the soldiers had blown it up to stop anyone else from using it – particularly the MacDonalds – when they departed for other battles around 1700. After the castles I had already viewed, Urquhart is a mere shell of its former self, in a spectacular setting nevertheless, but it took a great deal of imagination to see it as a living fortress. It has known a great deal of action, and all of this is outlaid clearly in both the information centre and in various notices around the ruins. Naturally I pulled myself up the uneven circular staircase to look out at the loch from the height of the battlements.

I followed the steady stream of people making their way back to the info centre and then the car park, eager to find my accommodation for the night. Just a little further along the A82 is the township of Drumnadrochit (I love saying that word!) and a short distance beyond that I encountered a farm sign with the words 'Drumbuie Farm B&B' at the gate. At the fence as I drove slowly up, I passed a gang of four frisky lambs, chasing each other, rushing to the fence together, staring at me over it, and then bouncing off as a group. They looked like trouble of a woolly kind.

My hostess met me at the door, and seeing the sign 'Urquhart Drumbuie Farm' I asked her if she was an Urquhart. Upon hearing she was Caroline Urquhart, I told he my own connections to the name, feeble though they were. We were off to a flying start. My room was a lovely spacious twin room with bathroom, overlooking the meadow and distant loch, the main road just visible down the hill. Be of all, just below my window was an idyllic pastoral scene of sheep, lambs, and cows all contentedly nibbling the grass, and the wee gang of teenage lambs were a lively part of that.

The guest part of this house featured a cosy sitting room complete with horned bull's head and a collection of books, and the dining room, which was a sweeping curve of windows over the meadow below, allowing a wide vista for every table. Caroline gave me a voucher for the hotel restaurant at the other end of Drumnadrochit, saying that her daughter worked there, so I set forth to find dinner at a discounted rate.

This town is quite pleasant with its proximity to the lake, the mountains and abundant in trees and carefully maintained setting. The main road is very busy, and road works were happening which slowed traffic down to a single lane when I was there. I found the

restaurant and was given a seat next to the bar, where I plunged into uploading my photos and post to the blogsite, sipping cider as I did so. Dinner was a sweet and sour crispy pork on noodles, and most enjoyable, despite having to overhear the three staff members behind me complain about their work and management.

I returned through the road works and past the frisky animals, to settle in for the night, still amazed at the brightness of the light although it was evening now. The rest of the evening was spent watching James Bond in 'Skyfall' (appropriately placed nearby in Scotland) to the sound of the odd bleat from outside.

Wednesday 3 June

Loch Ness to Tobermory, Mull

Breakfast this morning was a bucolic delight, sitting facing the pasture below and watching the inhabitants frolic and gambol about. One or two of the beleaguered ewes took to crouching on the grass chewing slowly, to avoid the constant attentions of their teenage lambs. But then these clever delinquents would jump on their mother's back and nibble at her ear until she stood up again, and they could nurse. After that, they found the rest of the gang, and sped off to the bottom field to roam the fence line, springing into a high leap every now and then.

A young and smiling Austrian couple occupied the other table, and I sang them my 'Droben in Oberland' song, in an effort to learn its origin, watching their eyelids peel back. Whether it is my singing, my accent, or my inaccurate translation, no one EVER claims it comes from their country, and yet it is so blatantly a beer-drinking song, Germanic in origin.

It was a bright day, with sunlight sparkling on the black waters of Loch Ness when I turned right from the drive and joined the traffic on the A82 south towards Fort Augustus again. Once I navigated through the busy convergence of roads at that town, I continued on that road, following the bead necklace of lochs towards Fort Willam. Somewhere up in the cloud cover to the left of the road just before reaching the town, is fabled Ben Nevis, rising majestically into the sky.

Approaching Fort William from the north, I stopped the car at a little car park on the end of the main street of town, right beside a monument with a stern-faced Highlander leaning on a cane. I felt I ought to make obeisance to Donald Cameron, 24th chief of the Camerons, but he didn't appear to notice me, thank the Lord.

Fort William

The main shopping street in this second-largest-Highland town, is set up for walking traffic with paving stones, cycle racks, and plenty of people. Despite seeing so much of the blue sky, it was breezy and not at all summery, and I darted in and out of the stores along this stretch eager to keep warm. These are old brown brick or grey stone buildings lining each side of the pedestrian mall, with occasional bursts of colour in modern facades. Nothing is higher than three levels, and many retain the air of antiquity about them. I posted postcards back to New Zealand in one of the red postbox pillars, and found a café in which to linger over my I-pad and sip coffee. I bought a hot pasty at one of the bakeries on my way back to the car, and set off for the Isle of Mull.

There are a few different ways to get to the island, all of them necessitating a ferry trip, and the most common seems to be to hop on a boat from Oban, thus saving some travel on the remote land of Morvern (almost an island in itself). From Fort William to Oban it is a little over an hour of driving, and thinking I would do that, I set off on the A82 again. All along this stretch of busy road

I followed the edge of Loch Linnhe, enjoying the sight of boats on the water, and the distant lands beyond the far shore. I came suddenly upon a signpost saying, 'Ferry to Corran' and made a quick change of plan: I blame all the traffic on the road, and the lure of the loch waters.

Just down the service road to the ferry ramp, a line of about six cars waited for a small car ferry I could see navigating a short stretch of water between the two docks. I got out to inquire of the woman in the car in front as to tickets and prices, and she very kindly gave me a return ticket from her concession booklet, considerably cheaper than the one I would have had to buy from the ticketing officer walking around on the ferry. (I later saw notices advising the need for proof that a concession ticket came from a book you own, but fortunately, my ticket was accepted, both ways.)

Soon I was driving up onto the almost-island of Morvern, and speeding along the open road through countryside apparently bereft of many houses, but wonderfully hilly, even mountainous, and quite a pleasure to drive through. (You might gather I do not enjoy being stuck in long streams of trucks and campervans on the main roads). I followed the signposts leading to Lochaline and the ferry terminal there, and arrived an hour later to descend the road in to this little town and join another queue for the ferry. Over the flat watery expanse ahead I could see quite clearly the shore and landscape of Mull, undulating and green/brown with some visible peaks. The thick clouds cast moving shadows over the tableau and I felt my excitement rise at going to another island of the Hebrides. I had not planned where I would be staying tonight, and so felt that thrill of the unknown doubly, watching the ferry nose across the mouth of Loch Aline and get swept into the current. A much larger ferry I recognised as being like the one I had taken to Harris glided past in front of us leaving a white wake behind her and heading towards the Western Isles.

At Fishnish (love the name!) we pulled alongside a sloping

ramp and the L-shaped platform on board lowered to much mechanical clamour, allowing us to disembark. Fishnish is not much more than a concrete slipway, built to serve the ferry, with a fast food place and public conveniences. The surrounds are mostly pine forest and the little road winds up through this a short way until it reaches a T-junction turning either left toward Fionnphort and the ferry to Iona, or right toward Salen. I turned right.

The initial part of this journey was hampered by roadworks but I had ample time to observe my surroundings change from pine to more open rolling countryside, and then a cluster of close buildings and houses as I reached Salen. Here I stopped to refill my car's empty tank and chat to the lady behind the counter about the best place to head for the night. She looked astonished that I would consider anywhere else but Tobermory, only another half an hour away in the direction I was going. I thanked her and continued my way, reaching enough height in the road that there were some lovely sweeping views out into the sea and distant ranges on the mainland. Puffy white clouds skidded across the sky, and the blue patch was getting bigger.

Despite having seen Tobermory on tourist sites online, I was unprepared for the absolute prettiness of this seaside town when I drove down the hill in to the waterfront area. The bright row of colours that each of these buildings was painted made them shine like jewels reflected in the little harbour they circled. The fact that most of the Highland houses I had seen before were white, only made these stridently coloured shops more dazzling for their uniqueness. To say I was delighted is an understatement. At the sea wall there is adequate parking for cars, and I was out in a jiffy and striding eagerly along the shop fronts, clicking photos as I went. Of primary importance in my mind was the need to secure accommodation for the night, and I saw that the first few buildings were hotels or guesthouses. Sadly, upon enquiring, I learned that they were all either full, or a lot more than I was prepared to pay.

One receptionist though, feeling for my plight, called a friend on my behalf who ran a B&B not far away. Sure enough, I was soon winding my way up to find the B&B on Dervaig Road (B882) for a mere £35 for the night. Now that I come to write about it, this is the only place I have not noted down anywhere, nor kept a business card from, and neither is it mentioned in any of the online directories. I suppose there needs to be one place in every story that remains a mystery, and this is it. When I drew in to the substantial car parking beside this modest two-storey home, it was already full of cars belonging to the teenagers in the family. My black-haired hostess, her round face surrounded by a mess of curls, met me at the door and said she would have them move the cars, and took me up the stairs to a room with twin beds, facing out toward the sea. I would be sharing a bathroom across the hall with one other, although I never saw them in the course of my stay. Two cushion-

less cane chairs sat beneath the window, and if I stood, I could see other houses built in the 50's and 60's just like this one, all with plenty of grounds and trees, and over the top of one of these, I could see the nearby ocean and the hills of Mull. I chose the least squeaky of the beds to lie down on and contemplate my next move.

Taking an alternate and less circuitous route down to the port, I zig-zagged down the road from the house along the narrow winding streets directly above the shopping area. Here I parked and with jaunty step started from the opposite side of town and began my investigation of Tobermory in earnest. Every shop window held much to fascinate a visitor from as far away as I had come. I took off my jacket and squinted into the sun, enjoying what felt like the first summer day since I had come to Scotland. Adding to that illusion was the sight of tourists walking

by with ice creams cones in hand, their arms swinging and wearing sunglasses. A ginger cat blinked up at me from a bookshop window, and so I was drawn in to finger the books in the shelves and enjoy the smell of print and paper. Going outside again, it was impossible not to feel buoyant, knowing I was by the sea and smelling fish in the air and the unmistakeable cries of seagulls.

I continued past the red, yellow and blue buildings at this end of town, loving the strong colours, and saw a station wagon parked on the road with 'Tobermory Otter Fund' emblazoned all over it. The side mirrors had toy otters attached, and there was a hole in the panel over the back for cash donations. I would LOVE to have seen an otter, and came close a few times in my travels, but not close enough.

My favourite store was a – well, I don't know what to call it – bottle store that sold telescopes? Toy store that sold hardware? Fishing store that sold whisky? They are all true. It was so fascinating the shop attendant stood back and let me take a panoramic photo on my camera, just so that I could fit it all in. Further on there was a café, small supermarket, gift shop, ice cream shop, and across the road by the boats, a caravan selling fish and chips. I asked a local store owner where the best fish shop was, and was told down the far end of town, but upon reaching it found it already closing, so I joined a group sunning themselves on the steps of the clock tower eating fish and chips from the little caravan instead. They were delicious. The fishing boat tied up in front of me was called 'The Dawn Treader' and just like Reepicheep, I could have said:

"My own plans are made. While I can, I sail east in the Dawn Treader. When she fails me, I paddle east in my coracle. When she sinks, I shall swim east with my four paws. And when I can swim no longer, if I have not reached Aslan's country, or shot over the edge of the world into some vast cataract, I shall sink with my nose to the sunrise."

— C.S. Lewis, The Voyage of the Dawn Treader

Naturally, after fish and chips, I finished my makeshift dinner with an ice cream, eaten while wandering along the rest of the shop fronts, into the pastel end of town. Picking up some light provisions from the supermarket, I was very happy to see that there, on Mull, were bottles of New Zealand 'Wither Hills' Sauvignon Blanc.

Back in my room, later, I got out my little book of walks on Mull and Iona, and plotted a route to take on the morrow that would allow for some hill climbing and walking. Certainly, if the weather was as fine as it had been today, I was sorely in need of some exercise, and I also had a bullet point on my Scottish bucket list that needed crossing off: 'Climb up a peak and take a deep breath.'

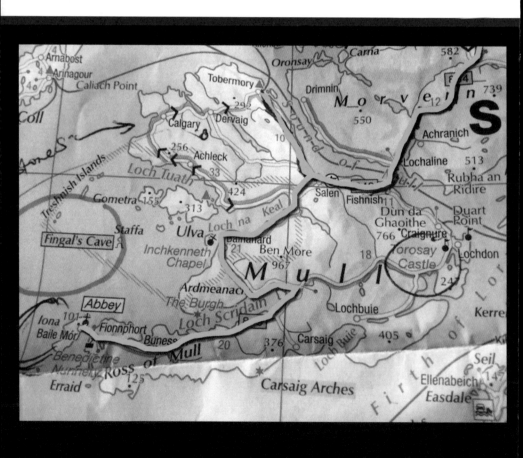

Thursday 4 June
Tobermory, Mull to Iona

The day started, like most of the others, in the dining room enjoying breakfast cooked for me by someone else. There were two staid older women at the other table who must have had their own bathroom, and were politely ignoring me.

I spent some time before leaving, unravelling my little backpack and filling it with some of the provisions purchased at the supermarket the previous night: muesli bars, fruit, water, chocolate, and of course my rain jacket, cellphone, camera, hat and gloves. I was going to finally 'peak' today!

I put on my heavy hiking boots, brought all the way from New Zealand and probably accounting for a large portion of the reason my bag tipped near maximum weight. I wore them twice.

My first stop was the information centre I had seen earlier, just past the Tobermory Distillery down on the waterfront. Steps led up in to what was a lightweight caravan, with a desk at one end, and walls full of pamphlets and maps. The floor of the info centre creaked under the weight of the tourists pressed in there, and I went directly over to the middle-aged woman waiting behind the desk wearing a wavering smile. In retrospect, I wonder if she was a last minute ring-in, but you be the judge.

Me: "I am hoping to climb up Ben More today, can you tell me how easy it is?"

Her: "Oh, it's a very easy climb – why, families walk up there all the time."

Me: "Oh, really? That's a relief, and here I was thinking it was going to be a haul."

Her: "No, no, it's not too bad at all, and just takes a few hours."

Me: "Is there a map of how to get there?"

Her: "Just take the turn off from Salen and (convoluted

description of farms, trees, houses, and a car park somewhere.)"

Somewhat encouraged, I tucked myself back in to my car, and gingerly pressed my heavy boots on the accelerator. The day was much cloudier than the previous, but not actually raining, which I took as a good omen.

The meandering road to Salen follows the coastline, and widens and narrows almost whimsically, with passing bays. At one point as I rounded the curve of a bay, I saw a silver van and a large group of people all standing together with binoculars trained on the sea. I stopped as soon as I could at the nearest passing bay and looked back toward them, some little eager hope in me wondering if they were an Outlander series film crew scouting for locations (I know, I know, what and why out here?) I realised soon after, that

they would be otter watchers, intent upon seeing the little critters, and I got back in my car and continued.

At Salen, a smaller road (if possible) separates from the main road, and veers off to the right, heading towards Loch na Keal, although all I could see from the road were scattered trees, some farmhouses, and stone fences. With my nose almost pressed to the windscreen, I kept a jaundiced eye on the growing dark shape of mountains ahead, most of which were now lost in low cloud. Even what I could see was so daunting I got out my I-pad and video-d my drive ahead, stone wall on the left, bluebells waving on the verge, but ahead, a monstrous shape rising out of the ground.

Looking back now, I suppose I was expecting a well-signposted car park and, perhaps, toilets, and clear signs of a path leading up the mountain – maybe even an ice-cream cart. Instead I scrabbled to recall all the details of what I had been told at the information centre, from the farmhouses just before the approach, to the car park at the base, and I found a few cars parked together, so I pulled in beside them, and got out to investigate. There was, indeed, a notice by a farm gate, which said 'Ben More Estate' and went on to describe a list of rules regarding sticking to the path and not diverging off on to the private land etc. Still unclear as to whether this was the track that took one up to the summit, I asked a couple of elderly gentlemen who were returning to their car, and they said they were not sure, having just come for the bird watching, but it was possible.

With fading enthusiasm, I pulled on my backpack and set off in the direction they had come, a smaller path that lead upwards. I was feeling a bit tired by the time the path wound down to join the road a little way ahead and was so obviously not heading up the mountain. Returning, I took the metal road that a recent 4-wheel drive had come down, (the notice said no public vehicles to go beyond the gate), so I assumed it had come from the farm. This flat metal road continued for some distance in towards a loch, and at the point where a cattle stop appeared between the fences, two young women with a pushchair passed me going back to the cars. (What? A pushchair!!)

On and on I walked, feeling the burn in my thighs, and the clanking of my pack, and I kept an eye on the steep slope beside me, hoping for sign of a clearly marked path leading up into what was now low cloud. I was questioning the wisdom of my decision to climb this peak, when the road gradually turned around the shoulder of that mountain, and ahead was the loch, and on the further side an even higher mountain rose into the sky. 'Disheartened' does not even come close to how I felt in that moment. That higher mountain must be Ben More. I was, in fact, only a half or a third of the way to the foothills of that monster ahead, and already feeling like I had walked five kilometres. (I hadn't, but my muscles had not been exercised on anything more taxing than brakes and clutch for a few weeks!)

I turned around and plodded miserably back along the rocky road, muttering under my breath some of the things I would have said to the woman in the information centre regarding 'family-friendly' and 'easy climb'. I also enjoyed my own little joke: "I'm going to conquer Ben LESS when I find it."

With my pack tossed in the back seat, and my lighter shoes on, I was soon singing along to Skipinnish and tapping my fingers on the steering wheel again, following the side of Loch na Keal on the 'scenic' route to Fionnphort, where the ferry would leave for Iona. There is nothing quite like NOT climbing a horribly steep hill in cold wet conditions to do wonders for the spirit.

A little further along the open pasture I came upon a stone arch bridge over a stream and a pleasant little scene of white farmhouse, ducks, sheep, colourful pot plants hanging on the walls and best of all, a sign saying 'coffee'. It was the easiest decision I've ever made to pull over and go through the door into a small cramped vestibule full of coats, boots, and a door to the toilet. From the hallway I could see the dining room was full of people and every chair filled and I was jostled back by a very flushed woman clutching a tray of drinks and toasted sandwiches. A man's voice behind me in the open door to the kitchen shouted some instruction to her, and I saw another man sitting amiably at the kitchen table sipping his own tea. Disappointed, I turned and started to make my way back to the door, when the woman returned and called out to me:

"Would you care to come and sit in here? There's plenty of room," and she indicated the kitchen table. The seated man stood and put a cap on and brushed past me saying it was time he was on his way anyway.

Yes, I would MUCH PREFER to sit in the kitchen – and so I eagerly made myself comfortable on the already warm wooden chair, and said I would love a coffee and a slice of the excellent cake I could see on the side

table. What a pleasure it was to sip coffee at that old wooden table, watching this husband and wife labour over their food preparation and managing to chat in between bursts of, "Just scrape the mould off, the cheese is fine!" or "Will you get me more bread from the freezer." They were probably the busiest B&B/café I visited in my travels.

And now we come to a stretch of road that was far and away the worst in my driving around Scotland. On the map, of course, it all looks just like so many fine green lines, but in reality it was a single track with occasional passing bay, and winding around coastline or marshy flat. At one point I was pulled in to one of those bays and another car came in behind me to let a large 4WD past. This vehicle being so large it was unable to get past both of us as the car behind was protruding out into the lane. The loud blonde woman who drove it rolled her window down and shouted at me: "You'll have to back up so that I can get around!" while I looked in amazement at her. The car behind found a bit more room and she was able to squeeze past, while we waited in some awe.[17]

Further around, and blessedly alone on the track, I saw the

17. It was only one of a few times that a driver of a more upscale gas-guzzling 4WD felt that my lesser car could back up to the next bay to let them by. I pretended ignorance usually and did not move. Hello!?!

road hugging the curving cliffs, the shore well below, and as if that was not enough of a hurdle, a small flock of ewes and lambs were wandering about. As far as I could see, there was no 'passing bay' sign, and each of the corners was blind.

So dangerous did it feel that I added to the tension by filming it – balancing my I-pad on the dashboard as I drove slowly ahead, hoping not to encounter a campervan coming the other way. A lamb scuttled around in front, following its mother down the bank, but apart from that, I made it safely to the land beyond and my heart went down into my chest again.

The road entered a broader valley and then climbed some hills, and finally joined a wider, busier road coming from Fishnish directly to Fionnphort. Glancing back in the rear vision mirror, I saw Ben More behind me, and wondered what on earth I was thinking to believe I could ever have scaled it.

The clouds had closed in, as I drove down toward the ferry, past a park filled with at least five coaches. Other cars were parked in a short-term parking area alongside and a crowd of tourists lingered around by a small building offering refreshments and timetables. A helpful official walking up toward the buses informed me that the long-term parking was back up the hill and around the corner, and so I turned and drove up there. The park was almost full of cars! The little island of Iona must be completely swarming with day-trippers like ants on an anthill and I was very glad I had booked to stay the night.

Another woman in a minivan recently returned from the ferry saw me slipping my pack on my back and since it was now raining lightly, offered to run me back down the hill, where she was picking up a large bag she had left at the ferry building. In my haste to take her up on the offer, I neglected to take my walking boots with me, which proved to be a very sorry oversight.

I huddled out of the rain amongst my bags in the tiny window seat next to the counter, enjoying watching the ferry approach, and the German tourists making selections from the cabinet. Not knowing any German, it was still possible to discern from facial expression and tone that many of the bakery items did not come up to Germanic standard, or were a mystery to them. I munched my excellent shortbread and sipped my juice in quiet amusement.

From the slipway standing waiting with a growing crowd of daytrippers and locals returning from work on the mainland, I could see across the water to Iona and appreciate the shape of the island. It was quite low and certainly green, dotted with those little square white shapes of houses or shops, and at the far right a rounded hump rose which I took to be Dun I (pronounced 'Done Ee'). Already I was readjusting my 'peak challenge' plans to a humbler level and seeing the mountain climbing not altogether lost.

The ferry backed in, and one or two local cars drove on while we foot traffic walked down the ramp and found seats inside. (The only vehicles allowed on the island are resident's cars, garbage trucks or those with a special licence to go there.) Twenty minutes later we were disembarking up another little ramp next to a line of dinghys, boat trailers, forklift and fishing buoys. The road divided into two, then went further up the hill and a parallel road came off it. I followed the majority of people up along the first turn on the right pulling my small wheelie bag along the rough surface of the narrow drive in front of some stately brown brick or white buildings. These all had gables and substantial front doors and pairs of windows looking out over the white sand beach further down. I was relieved to see that one of them said, 'Argyll Hotel' and pulled my bag and myself in out of the drizzle to shake myself off in the hall inside. Very soon a man in his fifties with a bright eye and bounce in his step greeted me and led me through to the dining room where the registration book was. My stay was costing me £70 for a single room, more expensive than many of the places I stayed, but it was a hotel and it was in a unique setting and there was very little competition to speak of. He led me up the stairs past the third

sitting room door, and into a long corridor from which rooms led off on either side. I had the choice of a single bed in a small room with bath and shower over it, or a single bed in a room with just shower, or he said, leading me up to the hall behind, I could have a single bed and just a bath but with a view toward the convent. The choices, the choices. I chose the view out back toward the convent and the deep bath option.

It was a relief to dispense with my luggage and set off to investigate Iona, and it was at this point I looked down and saw my cloth walking shoes, the tread worn so thin there was a split in the sole, and knew my boots were in the back of the car on Mull. I shrugged back in to my waterproof coat, put my little backpack on, and set off in the drizzle to explore.

Directly behind the rows of shops, hotels and houses are the ruins of the convent and it was there that I headed first. At times throughout my life I have read of Iona in the novels relating to early spiritual life in the Celtic world, and when I knew I was coming to Scotland, Iona was high on my list of 'must see's. Words will fall far short of describing my feelings in stepping in through the ruins of the cloister and reading the notice 'World of Women' just inside that gate. I am not a Catholic, but I am a Christian, and a single woman who has lived independently all my life, and I well know that for millennia women could not do that easily. It was moving to read:

The convent provided refuge for unmarried daughters, widows, illegitimate girls and estranged wives. Far from leading lives of poverty and seclusion, these women had daily contact with the outside world. They supported themselves financially, living off income from nunnery lands on Iona and beyond. Until the 1600s, the south shore of Mull's Loch na Keal was known as 'Leirnacalloch' meaning 'hillside of the nuns.'

It seemed fitting to start my wander of this island right here. This place was as skeletal as Urquhart Castle but the bones of the

different rooms and cloister were still apparent, as were the arched windows and doors that were all that remained of the small chapel. And somehow that musky pink brick in amongst lush green spring grass and daisies was very feminine in aspect. There were too many people wandering through with me, to be able to pause for long reflection, and so I moved on, vowing to return when they had all left. I poked around in one or two shops and in the information centre, bought a few postcards and a map at the tiny Post Office tucked down a narrow path near the Dock area, and then went back to my room for a rest.

I heard the unmistakeable sounds of the ferry departure an hour or so later, and feeling pleased that the rain had departed as well, I went up the narrow path beside the hotel and in through the extensive vegetable garden at the back. Beyond the Convent the road winds slightly up and along past the information centre and then along beside the broad manicured lawns of Iona Abbey itself. This is not a ruin but has been restored as recently as the early 20th century at the instigation of the 8th Duke of Argyll. It was here that so much of the religious life on Iona took place, and it has been used in the burying of kings, and a spiritual centre for centuries, at least as early as St Columba's arrival in AD563, when Christianity spread into Scotland. Further on from the Abbey the road continues to the northernmost point of the island, and rising like a blister out of the lush emerald land is a rocky hill that must be Dun I. In the foothills further back from the road was a beautiful white house with seven gabled windows along its upper floor. And just beyond the house I encountered a gateway leading into a field with the sign 'Footpath to Dun I'. Seeing the rocky peak ahead – certainly within my ability to climb – I lunged through the gate and squelched up the slope following a worn track in the grass toward the hill. I was almost alone – oh joy – just one person ahead of me cresting the slope, and I jumped from side to side of the indentation in the grass, avoiding puddles and sheep droppings, until I reached the Dun. My shoes had long since given up keeping my feet dry and I could feel the water seeping in over my socks.

The path appeared to go up a diagonal into a big collection of rock, with grass and moss filling cavities in the places the tumble of rocks came together, and allowing for myriad small streams to flow down in these clefts. It was actually harder than I expected to gain a firm footing, especially in my tread-less shoes, but I bent to the task, felt the water seep further around my toes, and slipped once or twice on the bare rock faces as I tried to avoid the soggy ground. A white face appeared briefly over the ridge of rock near the top, and then the person I had been following reappeared at some distance away descending by another way. Had they wanted

to be alone? Did they think I looked dangerous? I will never know. They did not make it to the top.

It may not seem much from the pictures, but Dun I was a good challenge for those who do not do a lot of rock and hill climbing: i.e. me. When I finally saw the stone cairn at the top, I felt inordinately exhilarated – as if I had indeed climbed a much higher peak. The view was impressive enough. I turned slowly 360 degrees feeling as if I stood alone in the middle of a vast ocean, and thinking of how old and strategic this island was, how vulnerable to those who had raided it, and yet oh, what a peaceful place it was at its heart. The Atlantic stretched on forever to the west, and in every other direction, the rough coastline and mountains and islands of Scotland filled the horizon. Down from the cairn is a rock with a dark pool beside it, which I had read was 'the fountain of youth'. Naturally, I ran my fingers through it. When I had drunk my fill of the view from the top and felt the night drawing in (the light would remain until after 10pm), I started to make my way down. It was much harder going down than it was coming up! When I thought I had a clear descent I would reach an edge and look over a sheer drop of cliff face, and so had to return and try elsewhere. An edge of panic crept in as I considered what I would do if it got truly dark and I was stuck up here. My feet were cold and wet, my shoes slipped into deeper swampy pools, the rocks moved as I walked on them, and for a while I was quite miserable. After a few false starts, I came upon a slope that I had ascended, and squished through it, finding at last the worn path in the field. When I arrived at the ruins of the convent, now empty of tourists, I was still feeling profound gratitude at having safely descended the 'mountain', and slipped very easily into a prayer as I stood in the shell of the chapel, (another of my bucket list points). Then I tracked slowly around the cloister singing softly under my breath, with the strongest sensation that I was following the steps of so many women who had done just this centuries before. It was a truly lovely moment.

I had no choice but to continue wearing my wet track shoes along the road and in to the cosy bar and restaurant at the far end by the slipway to the ferry. Seated inside sipping a cider provided by a gregarious Australian barman and feeling the success of my climb again, I logged in to my blog and uploaded the triumphant photos. No one but you and I, dear reader, know what that descent was like.

It became quickly apparent that almost everyone on the island was eating at this bar and bistro tonight – my own hotel restaurant was closed due to some double-booking – and the only other was the more expensive one near the Abbey itself. I was given a table in the middle of the room but could see clearly out on to the ocean, and feeling a great warm glow well up inside, ate a very tasty meal finished off with the best slice of pavlova I have ever had (courtesy of a New Zealand chef who was in the kitchen.) The friendly owner of the Argyll Hotel spotted me sitting there, and came over for a chat and to find out what my day had been like. He was awaiting his wife, and the two were looking forward to dinner together on a rare night away from their own establishment.

After stretching my meal out as long as I could, I reluctantly left the warmth of the bistro – they needed my table after all – and walked slowly back to my own room. The diffused light outside gave the impression it was still around 6pm but was closer to 10pm. I was feeling very tired and my shoes too wet to consider going out and roaming the island as I had anticipated I would when planning this visit from my studio back home. Here was the only opportunity to get out and see it without hoards of day-trippers and while the rain held off, but instead I ran a deep bath and soaked until I was almost asleep. I found just enough energy afterwards to soak my shoes and leave them drying over the oil heater before my head sank into the pillow.

Friday 5 June
Iona to Oban

My hopes to be awake in time to investigate the outer reaches of Iona before the day-trippers arrived were crushed upon waking to the sound of the ferry arriving. I pulled open my curtains and saw a steady drizzle had set in. It was a bit disheartening. Still, there was breakfast to be had downstairs, and I had a decent coat, if not shoes.

Out in the conservatory downstairs I munched my very good cooked breakfast watching people in raincoats and umbrellas push past along the road avoiding puddles. Many of them ducked in to the hallway of the Argyll, which served as a café as well and had a few lounges. Soon I joined the throngs outside, wearing my coat and my not-quite-dry shoes, which now additionally had a most unpleasant aroma. (Did the soaking release a few year's worth of accumulated foot odour? I shudder to think.) My bag was tucked in a cupboard to be picked up later.

I determined to go to the south and cross over the island to see the famous white sand beaches there, and so set off along the road in the rain. As I passed the bistro of the night before I noticed a sports store directly opposite and had a moment of inspiration. Before long I was dressed in some waterproof overpants and would have felt up for any weather, except that they did not sell galoshes. It was an easy walk along the roadway, making a loud nylon swishing sound with every step, and I tried not to notice the moisture creeping in under my soles. There were about seven or eight houses set back on sections along this road, and various farm animals in the paddocks on either side. A large garbage truck I had seen come off the ferry moved slowly past me to collect the rubbish put out at the crossroads ahead. I came to the end of the road and up against a farm gate, with a notice saying to keep to the path ahead. My heart sank: it was raining steadily, the ground was soggy, and I was still a good way from the sea that I could see in the distance over the paddocks. I made a half-hearted start across the field and felt the moisture gush in over my socks. In an instant, my motivation collapsed, and I turned and walked back to the gate. Instead of a photo of a sparkling azure sea on white sand, I have one of me in my raincoat pointing into the hazy grey distance at what would be the beach if I had gone there.

Feeling a little despondent I trudged back with rain batting my face toward the other coast, but had not gone far when an old car pulled up beside me, and the window wound down. "Would you like a ride to the shops?" a woman called from the other side. It was so odd to be offered a ride on Iona, where there must be about two cars, but I was not turning it down. I climbed in and we set off, but soon after the farmer (for that's what she was) turned on the internal fan with some force. Even I could faintly smell my unfortunate shoes from here, and was hoping it was not noticeable. (Perhaps she just didn't want to fog up the windows?)

There did not seem much point in lingering on Iona, since the bad weather had set in, so I took the next ferry back to Fionnphort, and eased happily back behind the wheel of my VW Polo.

I was a bit torn between returning for another night at Tobermory, which I loved, or going on towards Glencoe. When I worked backwards from the date I had to return the car in Bournemouth, I had to be in Glasgow by the day after tomorrow, and that decided me. One day I hope to return for a more lingering stay on Mull, which has some very beguiling mountains and long open spaces to walk or explore.

The road to Fishnish was pretty direct and I wasted no time

driving along it. At the ferry I approached the tiny fast food stall and purchased a hot chocolate to drink while I waited to catch the ferry back over to the Morvern area. I retraced the road I had taken on my trip to Mull, and the same little ferry awaited me at Corran. By early afternoon, I was on the very busy A82 that heads south to Oban or inland to Glencoe.

As if in response to my own lifting of spirits, the sun came out and although I intended to stay the night in Oban, on impulse I took the inland road via Glencoe just so that I could see this amazing stretch of the Highlands. My memory of the long valley the minibus had driven down during winter in 2012, as still etched on my mind. Back then the mountains were all white, and the road a black line winding through it. Today, with the sun out, they were a rich tapestry of browns, greens and mauve, and approached from the west they presented quite a different impression. The actual village of Glencoe was a disappointment, especially after all the traditional towns I had passed through recently, rich in history and community. This village seemed set up for the tourists who streamed through, on their way to enjoy winter sports in the mountains. When I found a little modern café tucked away in a suburban street, and stepped inside, it was crowded with that very kind of tourist and noisy with chatter and waitresses pushing through the narrow space between tables. Standing – ignored – by the counter I soon gave up and returned to my car, striking the village off as a place to linger in. I drove further along the road until I came to the very large information centre, museum, café and rest area, and although it lacked the warm ambience of a traditional tearoom, I enjoyed a hot drink and pastry looking out at the view. The car park, of course, was pay and display. The little museum inside required an entry fee. It is a well set up and informative space, though, and you would learn all you could need to know of this area, so rich in tragic history, by spending an hour or so here.

Out on the road I pulled over a few times just to gape at the

mountains again, and the incredible views between them leading down to the loch, or across to distant ranges. It is dramatic country and one feels very small standing in it.

Without planning it, I had taken on quite a bit of driving today, my route sweeping as far inland as Tyndrum, which brushes the Trossachs National Park, before returning out to the coast again at Oban. So I had the full benefit of seeing the fall of land from the mountains at Glencoe, through to the sweeping valley, rivers and forests of that central area above Loch Lomond. For once, the sky was a rich blue with puffy white clouds bouncing across it, and the grassy landscape bursting with spring colours. And I noticed another thing as I moved closer to the Trossachs: more and more cyclists on the road. In calling about accommodation for this evening, I had called some Glencoe B&Bs, and been told that there was a big event for cyclists this weekend and hence accommodation was at a premium. At least cycling in this area looked much more appealing than that which I had seen on Lewis, quite possibly because the sun was out and the wind had died away. (Something as simple as that can make a big difference to a leisure cyclist like myself.) I saw no leisure cyclists here; they were all clad in various layers of lycra and looked whippet thin.

I took the road west (A85) toward Oban at Tyndrum, and spent that hour enjoying the sunshine bringing out the colours of the countryside as I passed through. It was 5pm when I drove down into Oban, and since my phone could not pick up the internet, I was forced to rely upon driving around until I could find a place called Kilchrenan House, Corran Esplanade. To my horror, 'driving around' was not going to be possible, as I soon discovered when I turned left into the main street . . . which was full of stationary bumper to bumper cars all leaving work to go home. This was the first true rush hour I had experienced since leaving Auckland a month ago. In fact, if I had just continued through the roundabout coming down the hill, I would have been at my destination in five minutes, but the next hour was spent slowly moving through town and receiving the disagreeable news at a petrol station on the far side, that Corran Esplanade was at the end of the long snake of traffic I had just passed.

It was all right – after all, I had all the time in the world, and I was IN SCOTLAND! Halleluiah!

Sure enough, eventually I followed the road around and found the 'esplanade' and the sizeable three-storey mansions all set up as guesthouses along this stretch of the road. Kilchrenan House is a grey brick with yellow door and window features, lacy eaves, and fifteen windows overlooking the harbour. I parked my car around the back, and went inside, finding an older couple of women leaning back on a sofa sipping whisky, and the sunlight falling on the decanter and glasses waiting on a tray at the main desk. Things were looking up. The diminutive woman with a brown bob who suddenly appeared in front of me, chatting constantly, turned out to be one half of the couple that owned the place. With an air of great efficiency she had me signed in, zipped up, and on my way lugging bags up the stairs before five minutes had passed, with a promise of a free dram after I was 'settled'. We took the turn at the top of the stairs, and then turned again and headed all the way down to the back of the house, where the single rooms are. Mine was comfortable with a queen bed, and its own tiny bathroom: the sort you have to squeeze in to the shower in order to shut the door. Best of all, from the window I could see the sea if I stood close and looked left. My stay would cost me £70, but I reasoned I would go for a cheaper place in the next few days to make up.

Oban is perfectly situated on the harbour, and with its mixture of old buildings, fishing boats, abundance of restaurants and plenty of notices about theatre or music, an exciting place to discover. As I walked the streets in search of dinner, I passed the ceilidh house, and saw the word 'Skipinnish' beside it, and a penny dropped in my memory bank. In December 2012, when the minibus had brought that group of young people and my friend and me in to Oban for the night, we spent the night dancing a ceilidh at that hall, no doubt to the music of Skipinnish, who are based there. Since then, I have got to know them because Sam Heughan (who plays Jamie Fraser in 'Outlander') tweeted about them, and hence my purchase of the CD, and the thrill of dancing to them live at the UK Gathering.

I stood on one of the docks, and video-d the panorama of Oban, including the small party of people leaving on a restored sailing boat. Behind me the sounds and smells of a restaurant called 'Piazza' serving Italian food, and I went inside and found the place bustling with happy diners. A very pleasant hour ensued, eating a delicious 'Pollo alla Aglio' or Chicken linguine, looking through the silhouette of a couple at the window table directly ahead of me, out to the glistening port just beyond. (They probably had a slightly uncomfortable meal feeling my eyes upon them). The tan brick of the buildings was made even more golden by the evening sun and left a sheen of iridescence on the water below. When I stepped outside, the owner of the restaurant, learning that I was a tourist, pressed a large postcard in to my hand, bearing an old photo taken of Oban from this very spot.

There were a range of different sized sailing boats tied up at this North Pier, and strolling around looking at them was a perfect way to walk off the cramps of driving and an excellent Italian meal. I was disappointed to discover that Skipinnish were not playing that night, or I would have flung myself around the dance floor to their music one more time. Instead I settled comfortably in a deep armchair

at the guesthouse, and updated my blog, before I made a cup of tea and fell asleep watching the evening sun descend over the Firth of Lorn.

Saturday 6 June
Oban to Inveraray

The dining room downstairs overlooked the choppy waves and an island called Kerrera, whose flat-topped mountains rose out of the land catching the sun on their green slopes. What a perfect way to start the day, eating pancakes, and thinking of the journey ahead.

I planned to go south toward the fascinating area steeped in ancient history involving stones, cairns and king-crowning hills, and was not too disheartened when the rain started as I drove along the main road of Oban. The first thing on the agenda, though, was to buy some replacement walking shoes! The pair that had literally died on Iona, were sending an invidious odour around the car, whether I wore them or not, and they needed burial. Knowing that on Saturday, most shops would not open until 10am, I was delighted when I saw a sportswear shop open as I drove past . . . and beside the shop, a car park space. There were only a limited range of styles and sizes, because the shop catered for clothing and equipment as well, so I was reaching desperation when we found a pair of waterproof men's shoes on sale. Feeling very pleased with myself, I strode outside in my grey and orange 'Oban walkers' (as they would forever remain in my mind), and finding a nearby bin, I tossed the old pair in with relief and a pang. After all, it was this very pair that had carried me up to the top of Rangitoto in Auckland harbour on the 'My Peak Challenge' weekend, and faithfully supported me through my Scottish trip so far.

I travelled south of Oban on A816, a winding but busy road that follows the contours of the land and after crossing countryside descends to Kilmore at the northern edge of Loch Feochan and hugs the coastline for a while. Seeing the glorious vista of the Loch ahead as I descended a steep hill, and a pretty glade with a store advertising café as well, I pulled in behind the shop. The door at the café entrance was shut, so I walked down and in through the front door, to find a small general store stocked with staple items of food, which served also as post office and newspaper distributor. A few locals were conducting transactions of the latter nature with a teenager who was clearly the only staff. When I asked over their heads about the café, she indicated some stairs at the back for me to go up and I found myself alone in a newly refurbished room, complete with counter, coffee machine and a few tables. A small amount of baking sat in the cabinet. Soon I heard steps coming up from down below and the same teenager went behind the counter and asked what I would like. I ordered my usual latte with an extra shot, and a biscuit, and paid. The young lass appeared to be flummoxed by the coffee machine, and said it was her mother's idea to have a café and she was not here right now. Some machine noises ensued, and I was given a small cup with black coffee at the bottom, and then she headed downstairs to learn how to make the froth work, ascending soon armed with that knowledge. It wasn't until I received another cup of milky coffee, that I realised I had a latte – and an extra shot in front of me. They were just not in the same cup. She was clearly feeling the pressure of her varied duties, so I merely joined the two liquids together, and smiling, sipped the lukewarm drink.

Just where the road turns sharply to go inland, there was a sign at Kilninver pointing out 'Seil' – a place my friend Fiona had encouraged me to see. Immediately I pulled off the main road and on to a typically narrow country lane (B844) that wound across some rugged countryside before approaching a remarkable single-arched stone bridge. When I drove up the narrow steep arch of the bridge and over the top – seriously, you cannot see what is coming from the other side – I had just crossed the only bridge over the Atlantic Sea. A humble little white-washed building welcomed me to 'The Isle of Seil', and I was fascinated to learn that it had been 'used by islanders after the Jacobite Rising of 1745 to change from their trousers into the forbidden kilt when returning to the island.' This particular bridge had been built in 1791. Standing in puddles in the cold showery weather, I hardly needed the final admonition on the notice that said, 'NO PICNICS IN THE CARPARK PLEASE.'

The island is not that large, but has a few tidy settlements of white croft houses, some stores, and much of the land is divided into hilly fields holding cattle or sheep. I drove slowly around just enjoying the view from my car and then doubled back and felt the thrill of excitement at lurching over a single-lane bridge without knowing if a bus was coming the other way. It was – but it waited on the other side for me.

I ploughed on down the wet A816, windscreen wipers squeaking, knowing I was passing some very interesting landmarks, such as the Craignish peninsula, 'Ardmaddy Castle' and 'Arduaine Gardens'. Down this area of the countryside it was definitely going to be a case of 'spoiled for choice', but I had my sights set on Kilmartin, a place so steeped in prehistoric monuments and historical sites, that I would be tripping over them as I stepped out of the car.

The road wound up into the pretty village of Kilmartin, set

up on a hill and rich with hedges and trees. It was also very busy, and I squeezed my car in beside others in the car park by the info centre, and wandered in to browse the shelves, learn something of the history here, and – had I not already just eaten – refresh myself at the well-stocked café. I purchased a felted brooch made out of the rare wool of a Soay sheep, which has prehistoric origins, armed myself with a collection of useful maps and pamphlets, and ducked the heavy raindrops back to my car again. It is embarrassing to admit, now that I am writing up my memoirs, that in researching some of the places I went to, I have discovered that I missed many a rare historical wonder. That includes Kilmartin Castle, which stands above the village in its newly restored state, and Carnassarie Castle, just further north. (Still, I have to leave some things to be discovered on a later trip.)

I drove down out of Kilmartin, and on to the flat land below the town, where the 'Nether Largie' standing stones were situated. Sure enough, with a surge of excitement, there they were out in the middle of a field, and I skipped lightly over the footbridge to investigate. This was when my new Oban walking shoes really came into their own: the track was waterlogged, the stream had long ago overflowed its banks so that buttercups bloomed below the surface, but oh joy, my feet were dry!

These standing stones were spread in formation some distance apart from each other, according to the notice, 'lining up with the rising and setting of the Moon and Sun at significant times'. Lacking either moon or sun to help, I rose and – lining up my I-pad – set it up so that it took a selfie of me reaching out to the biggest stone. Then I splashed back to the car park, observing as I went some stalwart walkers who had made a day of it, and were walking around the area between all the sites, bless them. Just a little further on, as I whistled along to Skipinnish, I glanced to my right and saw another paddock with toothy stones jutting out from it. (Sorry, I didn't stop . . . there's only so many stones you can see in a day.) It did serve to reinforce my awareness that there are over

350 ancient monuments, almost half of which are prehistoric, in this area alone. No wonder people were walking it.

The road entered a long straight, and I whizzed along it, but seeing a small green hill poking up in the middle of the plain, I realised I was looking at Dunadd, the capital of the ancient kingdom of Dairiada, and the 'king-making hill'. A sign confirmed my suspicions, and I turned off the main road and down the side road towards the hill. At the base of the hill was nestled another of those white croft houses, and a small footpath could be seen winding up towards the summit. Little capering figures were moving agilely

along the skyline up there, and I watched them for a moment. A spatter of rain over my windscreen, and suddenly I was pulling out and turning back to the main road, thinking of the ancient kings who had been taken up there to be crowned – probably in weather just like this. (I suppose I should call this book, 'A lazy kiwi's guide to seeing Scotland.')

How I wish I had another month to investigate all of the islands and peninsulas along this stretch of the coast alone! I felt that familiar pull as I reached the road (A83) that turned off into the expansive Kintyre peninsula – as big as Skye it looked on my map. It was this area that is the lyric in 'Mull of Kintyre' and not Mull, as I formerly thought.

I stayed on the A816, reaching the southern point at Loch Fyne and hugging the coastline up the western side of this large expanse of water. There were a few towns of good size up this coast, two to three-storey buildings forming a wall of shops and houses in shades of white, beige and brown. Busy though the road was, it was a pleasant drive through forested slopes, with regular views of the dark waters beyond. I had not booked accommodation for the night, and kept an eye on B&B signs as I passed them, but wanted to see if there was a place in Inveraray I could stay first. I am so glad I did.

Before long I came out from forested road and saw a township ahead, and on the outskirts a sign saying 'Inveraray'. The first I noticed were mansions set back on grassy lawns, facing the water, and most with elegant Guesthouse or Hotel signs at their gates. I continued on, until I reached the first rows of attached houses, noting first that they were all white, but attending more importantly to the odd B&B sign. All three of the places along here had no vacancy or no single room. I drove around a corner and on to the main street and was astounded: this place was gorgeous. Every one of the buildings was white with slate roofs: shops, restaurants and churches, and at the end of the road, the harbour. I found parking through some stone arches, pay and display of course, and set off for the tourist office. Here, a young lady called a few places on my behalf, and finished with two possibilities, neither of them in the town itself, and both £45. She was clearly keener for me to take the B&B furthest out because they were registered with the Tourist Office, and when I said I would take the closer one, she warned me that they could not guarantee the condition of this one, as it was unregistered. To fortify myself, I walked up to a café that had the most delicious range of cakes in the window, and sat down to a great 'flat white' coffee and Victorian sponge.

I drove back along the road I had come in from, going south again about 3 miles, until I reached a sign I recognised simply saying, 'Claonairigh House'. It was not a large sign, and hand painted, and all that was visible from the road was a rough drive leading away into the woods and fields beyond. Cautiously I nosed the car down here, and came to a gate leading off on the left, and a tall cream-painted brick house: another Lallybroch. It looked so splendid that I stopped and took photos. I parked and knocked at the side door, which was answered by an attractive pony-tailed lass in her teens, who welcomed me in, saying her mother was out but she would show me around. My mouth was agape as I passed the little vestibule, filled with little knick knacks, and then the entry hall, with its sideboard and books, and directly ahead a wooden staircase that we took, winding upwards to the third floor and what had once been the attic. On the way up there were old original illustrations from Winnie the Pooh framed on the walls, and at the top a sloping door lead to either of two rooms tucked under the roof. When I was shown in to my own space, leaning to get under the door, it was a little jewel of a room, painted reflex blue, with blue and white curtains and bed covers on the twin beds. A little fireplace held a row of pipes, and the bed heads had images burnt into them from The Hobbit. I was in the Lord of the Rings bedroom I discovered – definitely a home away from home. Another door in my room led into the bathroom, decorated in blues and whites, with a skylight in the shower out of which I could see the surrounding countryside.

There was even a vase of bluebells and dewdrops on the windowsill. When I had settled in, I went downstairs to the family dining room, which was where we would have breakfast the next day, and was given a pot of tea to enjoy. As if I could contain any more joy, I discovered this was the oldest building in the Inveraray area, built in [18]1745 by the Duke of Argyll for his Laird, and set in seven acres of gardens. I felt I had walked through the stones, myself, into the Scotland that Claire discovered.

I drove back in to Inveraray to see this exquisite little town, knowing now something of its history. The third Duke of Argyll demolished the existing castle in 1744 and spent the next 40 years constructing a new one, an architecturally designed Georgian mansion house that is still called a Castle. The fifth Duke rebuilt the town so that it matched the attractiveness of the castle, with a number of buildings architecturally designed. Today, the buildings must be kept in their present colour and state, and thus provide a glimpse into a former century and lifestyle. When I had exhausted my browsing, I went over to the 'George Hotel' at the top of the main street and was ushered in to their dining area in a huge conservatory at the back, which had flagstone floor, dark wood panelled walls and ceiling, and a lot of custom. Not feeling too hungry, I ordered two starters for dinner, and they were both melt in the mouth: scallops and bacon on a pea mash, and pork belly with cabbage, finishing with bread and butter pudding. Busy though the restaurant was, I certainly did not feel in the way, or rushed, and enjoyed the convivial atmosphere that surrounded me.

I found my way back along the country road and driveway to Claonairigh House, taking in the shells of the croft houses where workers on the farm once lived, and then climbed the stairs to my little haven. How I wish I could have stayed for longer! I heard the distant sounds of other guests arriving and going in to the room on the other side of the roof, but I lay awake reading, writing, and just soaking up the atmosphere, trying to stay awake as long as I could. It was heaven.

18. For Outlander fans, it is also two years after Claire walked through the stones into the Highlands.

Sunday 7 June
Inveraray to Glasgow

I felt a little sorry to be leaving for Glasgow today, for it marked the end of my trip around the Highlands. As well, I would have to relinquish the little room I had enjoyed so much. But I finally got to meet Fiona, my hostess and the mother of the two teenage girls who had been so friendly, and we greeted each other warmly down in the dining room. The fire was lit, the big polished wooden table was laden with preparations for breakfast, and through the kitchen door I caught glimpses of a room I would have spent hours in, had I the opportunity. A French couple were seated already at the table, and eyed me a little cautiously, not responding at any length to my polite enquiries about their travels, so I gave up. The cooked breakfast was great, and it did give an air of inclusion for us all to be seated at the big table together, although it took the arrival of a gregarious couple from America for the conversation to really

pick up. I noticed, somewhat resentfully, that having another male to talk to, made the Frenchman almost voluble, but it freed me to lean back and enjoy the rich ambience of this furnished family home.

When I left shortly after, Fiona and I exchanged Twitter and Facebook addresses, and I now enjoy keeping up with the life in her family through social media. She is an avid Outlander fan as well, which helps.

Fiona had told me that her daughter worked at the

Auchindrain Museum a few miles further south on the same road, and she encouraged me to go and see it. The car park was empty when I arrived and I remained the only visitor, somewhat startling the woman overseeing the office and shop when I opened the door. Auchindrain is an old communal farming village, like the many that were swept away after the Highland Clearances, but this one was still occupied up until the 1960s. Most of the old croft houses have corrugated iron roofs that replaced the thatch in the last century, but the village still bore something of the life that once lived here. I absolutely loved it: standing in a barn or a croft kitchen, smelling peat and having the distinct feeling people had just slipped outside to milk the cow or something. In fact, the farmhouses had a notice inside the door when you went through, with the name of the farmer who owned it and something of his family history. In the barn, the straw in the corner looked as if it was the very straw the last farmer - Stoner – had stacked, before he left his croft for good. I could easily imagine the community gatherings under that low ceiling.

Loath to leave Inveraray without a final walk down the main street, I stopped when I drove through the town, and entered the café I had enjoyed yesterday for a coffee. Then it was onward and downward toward the mighty city of Glasgow, following the A82 as it wound up and down toward Loch Lomond and then following the 'bonny bonny banks' of that lake to pass beneath its southern tip. This was part of the Trossachs National Park, which stretches right up to Tyndrum, where I had been a few days ago, and across east to Callander, where I had stopped on my journey north to Inverness a couple of weeks earlier. What struck me about Loch Lomond was how its mountains were stately, rather than enormous, the surrounding countryside soft with trees and lawns, and the lake busy with water sports of all kinds, even on this grey day. On a day when the sun was out, I am sure it would be dazzling. Compared to the mystery and drama of Loch Ness, Loch Lomond was gently refined.

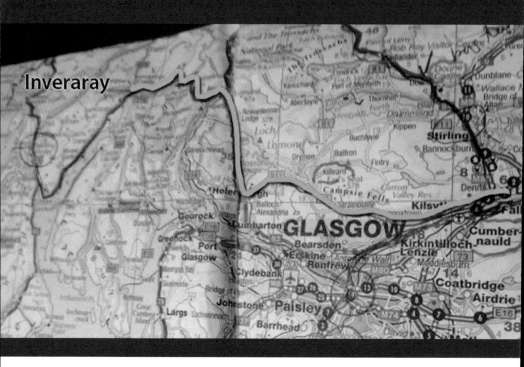

Inveraray

It is only an hour and a half from Inveraray to Glasgow, and my social media messages this morning had been lively with news of a gathering of some of the UK Outlander fans at Callendar House, in Falkirk, for lunch in the tearooms there. My memories of Falkirk had not been good, (when I stayed at the Antonine Hotel), and I had not seen another Outlander for weeks, which is what decided me to adjust the direction on my I-phone GPS. I skimmed the edges of Glasgow and continued east on the M80, and in half an hour, at around 1.30pm, arrived in the car park of a gracious park of lawns, gardens and old trees.

My expectations were that I would find all the ladies at a kiosk or band rotunda sipping tea in the middle of this park, and that Callendar House was probably one of the grey concrete buildings at the gates. How wrong you can be! With that in mind, I strode along the neat pathways, enjoying the rhododendrons and the sun filtering through the new leaves overhead. When I found a kiosk serving ice-cream I did not find the ladies, and so I continued along the path.

Not for the first time on this trip I was about to have my

expectations so far exceeded as to be ludicrous. Around a bend in the path ahead, I watched in awe as a pink-grey turreted mansion, like a fairy palace, emerged from a setting of sweeping lawns and broad driveway. This, then, was Callendar House. Feeling humbled and chagrined I entered the foyer and enquired at the desk about a group of ladies come for lunch. They informed me that the tearoom had not opened until 2pm, and it being that time now, I ascended the curved staircase to go in through a door in the wood panelling on the first floor. A few heads turned from the one or two tables occupied, but none were Outlanders. They must have arrived at 1.30, found it closed, and gone off somewhere else. I was just considering my next move, when a body of people emerged from a tour of the kitchens, and a voice called out my name. It was Nan, who I had met at the UK Gathering – in fact, looking around, I recognised most of them from that weekend. Before long we were jostling merrily upstairs, talking and laughing as we went in through some double doors on the first floor. Slightly bewildered, I saw that there was more than just lunch planned, for as I seated myself on the edge of a semicircle of seats, a young highland dancer took the floor and stood waiting with hands on hips and toes pointed. She was the daughter of Elaine, one of the Outlander UK administrators, who had organised the event, and she leapt and kicked nimbly through two traditional Highland tunes.

Then a bearded man in knitted vest and well-worn jeans stood and introduced himself. He was Geoff Bailey, 'Keeper of Archaeology & Local History' and he proceeded to outlay the history of the House during the Jacobite period. It was infinitely preferable to reading a brochure, for he injected his stories with humour and actions, and his passion was infectious.

We had worked up an appetite after these presentations and made our way through to the tearooms for the delayed refreshments. I sat at a lively table, between Sheila and Nan, in what could have passed for the dining room in Downtown Abbey. This was a great

opportunity to make up for the lack of friendly conversation in the last couple of weeks, and we bubbled with mirth and chatter for the next hour. I was very glad I had made the detour to meet up with these ladies. I left before they finished, waving goodbye to the whole room, all of whom had been made aware of my parting, poor things.

It was now just a simple matter of putting the address of the Mercure, Glasgow, in to my I-phone GPS, and heading in that direction. How hard could it be? I confess that after weeks of driving through quiet backwaters or the Highlands, and the remote islands, I was a little nervous of navigating the second largest city in Scotland. Half an hour later I was gliding in the traffic through the congested streets of early rush hour, and feeling quite pleased with myself when I heard the Google-map voice say, "Your destination is on the left." Yes, there was the sign and front doors for the Mercure Hotel, but wait, where was the parking I was promised? There were parked cars at the kerb, and nowhere to stop the car, so I took the first street left and pulled over when I could. I will spare you, the reader, the convolutions of the next hour, but they involved phone calls to the bored reception staff, negotiating unfamiliar streets to find the parking building, finding a park, and wheeling both bags over uneven pavement to the Hotel. Since I was paying more than I had paid at any other place in this trip (apart from Culloden House, which deserved every penny), I was disappointed to find the hotel was modest, scruffy, and with tired furnishings, and my room on the fourth floor a pokey corner overlooking the filthy walls of an inner courtyard. Lest I sound too negative, bear in mind that I had been somewhat spoilt by my previous accommodations and was feeling tired and alone in the big city. I soon perked up though – my new friend, Fiona, was meeting me downstairs, having travelled in by train from her home for the evening. (This is the same generous soul who met me in Edinburgh, and spent the day showing me around.) She was waiting when I got down to the foyer, and after our joyous hellos, we set off up the street towards the railway station and a hotel that had a good cocktail lounge. In stark contrast to Edinburgh, whose delightfully cobbled-together buildings are predominantly grey stone, Glasgow's are warm tones of brown or beige, and it is much less hilly. We strode up the pavement, enjoying the early evening crowds and the 'buzz'. Upstairs at the cocktail bar, we perched by the window, and sipped our pink champagne, feeling just as bubbly as we caught up on the last few weeks. It was a great pleasure to have company again.

Our plan for dinner was to take a recommendation that Sam Heughan himself had made on Twitter, and discover what dining at the new Gusto Glasgow restaurant was like. After watching their own marketing on Twitter and supporting them, it was great fun to actually walk through the double doors and be seated at a booth. The restaurant is large with lots of comfortable booths and mirrored walls, and the staff super-friendly. I ate a Rigatoni Primavera with chicken that I enjoyed very much, (despite my usual messy pasta-twisting technique.) I finished with the Strawberry and Passion Fruit Mess, which was almost like a pavlova. Naturally, we tweeted jubilantly about being there and received response from friends as well as the restaurant.

We picked our way back through the streets to the Railway Station in the bright twilight and parted company, but not before I received an enthusiastic response from Fiona about joining me the next day. What would we do in Glasgow for a full day?

I walked past the now-familiar statue of the Duke of Wellington sitting on a steed, who suffered the indignity of having to wear an orange road works cone on his head. (Apparently any effort to remove it lasted mere hours before it was restored. He was destined to suffer this ignoble fate for the foreseeable future.)

Back in my room, I made a cup of tea and lay on the queen-sized winding down in front of television. I remember waking a few times in the night to the loud shouts of voices swearing and remarkably loud, coming from the alley beneath my window and augmented by the walls above.

Monday 8 June - Glasgow

I woke and showered, and despite being disturbed by passers-by during the night, set off down to breakfast with a spring in my step. It was a bright summery day outside, and I was a little surprised to see how busy the street-level dining area was. It was not, after all, a back packers paradise as I had assumed, but a convenient place in the heart of the city for businessmen and women to stay,

as evidenced by the clientele who packed the buffet area beside me. Still, I am not persuaded that better places for the same money do not exist somewhere there. (My advice: keep looking).

The breakfast buffet was well stocked, and I sampled a good bit of it, before returning to my room to prepare for the day on foot. Wary of the changeable weather, I dressed in my usual long black polar-fleece pants and warm jacket, and set off towards George Square. There, waiting for me in light summer capris pants and a bright blouse, was Fiona. (My own capris pants that I had worn around Edinburgh were tucked deep in my suitcase.)

I had wandered around the Square for a while, trying to discern which door Claire and Frank had strolled swinging their arms through, to their wedding, in Episode 1. Fiona led me around

Below: Frank and Claire in Outlander

the corner to the immense three-arched gate and just beyond, there the doors were, with the number 45 embossed on the side. Of course I strode out towards the camera, mimicking one of my own memes.

It was a great day to wander, the sun was out, everyone else was at work, and there was so much to see. Walking up toward the Glasgow Royal Concert Hall, we came to an intersection and a waist-high plinth with a beautifully rendered bronze 3D map of the city. The two of us leaned over it, picking out where we were, and some voices just to our right whose backs were turned to us, intruded upon our viewing, so Fiona asked them to move over or something. To her consternation and my great amusement, they were the backs of two persons holding a microphone and filming an interview with another young chap. They ignored us, and the subsequent chortles, but I like to think that in some vital bit of news reporting somewhere Fiona's strident voice can be heard in the background accompanied by Kiwi accented laughter. We settled ourselves with a coffee at a nearby Starbucks, and then continued the 'rampage'.

In recalling my adventures around the city, I cannot now name the streets, or the particular direction we took, but it did take on a familiar feel over the course of two days. We walked up and down and at one point discovered the door into Scottish Youth Theatre, which is supported by Sam Heughan, (who obviously benefited from the same himself in the past.) We would have been happy to attend a show, but were told that it was a school and that no particular production was on at the time. Fiona and I had to make do with our own small production: an artistic reflection of ourselves against the window.

There was much to enjoy in the architecture as well – some sumptuous domed buildings with finials and arches, a LOT of noble persons in statue well above my head set in their own arched alcove amongst Corinthian columns, gorgeously embellished stone and brick buildings, with all the detail that gave them an air prestige a few centuries ago. Stepping away from the old buildings for a moment, the two of us went up an escalator into the delicately arched and filigreed atrium of Princes Square. The sunlight beamed down through the glass ceiling, illuminating a few tiers of shops and eating places, and the whole effect was of being in an oversized conservatory.

Our destination in the afternoon was to be the Kelvingrove Art Gallery and Museum on Argyll St, and we took the Subway (SPT) that runs in a circle under the city, to get there. After my experiences on both the Underground in London, and the Metro in Paris, this was a distinctly cleaner – if a much smaller – train line. In fact, the orange carriages were just tall enough for me to stand up in, and all looked quite new.

Kelvingrove is just past the University, a huge square red brick building built in 1901, with arched windows, verdigris spires, and regal entryways – all set in a grassy block with car park and trees. On the corner of this block is another plinth with a deeply embossed map of the city on it. We walked through the entry foyer and more glass doors to a bewildering array of choices directly in front of us. Well, actually, an elephant stood directly in front, with a wildebeest and a giraffe, and a Spitfire flew overhead, but I digress. It is definitely a place to spend a full day in. We did not have a full day, so I walked past the animals and museum, and made my way up the stairs to the art galleries, Fiona letting me follow my whim on this my first trip. Everywhere I walked my eye was drawn to some new novelty: more than fifty floating white heads bearing every possibly expression hung from the centre of the atrium, skulls and swords and silver sailing ships were set into alcoves of cabinets. The galleries were hung with paintings according to their era, and I stood before Salvador Dali's famous oil of a crucifixion hanging over a world, enjoying seeing his work up close at last. I was moved by the old Scottish paintings depicting the troubles the country

has gone through, and the glory of the landscape I so recently traversed. Eventually, the effect that all galleries and museums have on me, took hold: I had reached saturation point and could take no more in. Down we both went to the café on the ground floor, and here I partook of another Scottish first: a bottle of 'Irn Bru,' the national soft drink, a glistening orange gold beverage composed mostly of sugar.

On our walk back toward the centre of town, we stopped at a window overlooking the central Rail Station, offering a rather splendid view of the city.

Back in the main street I parted company with Fiona, and we hugged each other farewell and set off in our different directions; she to her home, and I to the Mercure. I had a duty to discharge, a burden to unload, a hope to see fulfilled. What was it? For the weeks preceding my trip to Scotland a huge card I had created to be given to Sam Heughan had been posted around New Zealand, being signed by Outlander fans in the main centres and containing an invitation to the country for he and Caitriona Balfe. (On a Q&A Facebook with him, when asked if he would come to NZ, he had said, "Where is my invite?") I had carried this around in the bottom of my suitcase along with some gifts, and had tried once, unsuccessfully, to deliver it. This afternoon would be my last opportunity.

With sweaty palms I tucked the plastic envelope and gifts under my arm, and headed out to find my car, and then I drove to the studio for the second time, and parked. My reception this time was less warmly received than the first time, but I handed the items over, hoping they would, indeed, reach Sam, along with the note attached to the outside. Task fulfilled, it was with a heavy heart I returned to my car, knowing that I would never get the first bullet point on my Scottish bucket list ticked off (to meet Sam Heughan and get a photo with him), but totally understanding why.

That return drive to Glasgow in my black Polo, was the

darkest hour of my whole trip, and I wallowed in it for about as long as it took to go through the doors of the hotel and fall onto my bed for a short rest. When I aroused to go off in search of dinner I was already feeling a bounce in my stride.

What I decided I needed to perk up fully, was a sizeable drink, some junk food, and lively music and chatter, and I found all of these in a restaurant called, appropriately: 'TGI Fridays'. In amongst a moving mass of young people, I squeezed into a table, tapped my feet to the background beat, and consumed a wicked amount of burger and fries, washed down by the biggest frozen margarita cocktail I have ever seen. It was a perfect remedy for the blues. As the night faded into darkness I sauntered through the neon lights and mauve sky, past the Duke of Wellington and his coned head, and in through the doors of the Mercure. If the inner courtyard echoed with cries and shouts in the night, I did not wake to hear them.

Tuesday 9 June
Glasgow to Wigtown

There was no need to rush today, so I took my time breakfasting downstairs and packing my suitcases again, careful to keep the overnight things in the smaller bag. I was going to go into the 'Lowlands' today, for my last night in Scotland, before heading all the way to Bournemouth by Friday. Checking out the possible routes on my disintegrating map, I looked for Wigtown that I had been encouraged to go and visit, where an Outlander by the name of Deborah ran a guesthouse. Seeing it was in the far south, and curious about a town calling itself 'The book town of Scotland', I sent a tweet to Deborah to see if her guesthouse had a vacancy. She tweeted back that it did, and although the single room was already taken, she said I could have the twin room. The other distinction her guesthouse had, was that Diana Gabaldon had also stayed there for a book signing event in Wigtown, and so for the second time in my trip, I was following in the author's footsteps.

The sun was still out when I stepped out onto Ingram Street and turned right, heading to find Glasgow Cathedral. I passed the City Halls and turned up some back streets going gradually north, and as I entered the outskirts things became more dilapidated and people looked more . . . edgy. A couple in rough clothing with hard faces and shifty eyes, darted a glance at me and the smile died on my own face. Two people smoking in an alley, looked sourly at me, and flicked ash on the ground. I might have just passed the area at a bad time.

That moment of transitory discomfort passed the minute I crested the hill and saw the buildings ahead, the first St Mungo Museum of Religious Life and Art, and the second the Cathedral itself. Impressive though the Museum is, with its unique shape, tower and windows, and the pale stone walls, I was here to see the Cathedral, and sat for a while on a seat in the sun looking at it. This

263

medieval building with its blackened bricks that only serve to add to its sense of vast age, looms over its cobbled courtyard. Everything about the outer structure begs examination, from the double doors deep inside a carved archway, the higher arch of the leadlight windows above, the lofty spires of different heights piercing the heavens. With my eyes gazing high overhead I almost missed the movement of the white vans on the left and work crew moving about behind temporary barricades. Yes, Outlanders, you read that right! This would mark the fourth time I came close to rubbing shoulders with the actors I would dearly have liked to meet. The t-shirts being worn by a few were 'Outlander Crew' shirts, and I knew I had stumbled on to a new location – probably the 'hopital' where Claire works in France. I restrained the impulse to tweet my find,

and merely enjoyed walking around seeing the activity and noting the people working downstairs in the temporarily closed off section. It brought a smile to my face to overhear one of the Cathedral staff speaking to a friend out enjoying sun on a bench beside me, that 'it was closed off downstairs for a film or something – terribly inconvenient.'

The inside of the building, naturally, was more ornate, with sumptuous details like the wooden arched ceiling with little icons on every crossed angle, and tiers of staggered arched windows, intended to draw the spirit of worshippers up into the heavenlies. And the stained glass windows – I have no words to describe how wonderful they are to see with a bright day shining through them. It is always refreshing to sit for a while and let yourself be uplifted if by nothing else, the sheer volume of artistry and skill that has created such a building.

When I felt I could linger no longer, I reluctantly left the area to return to my car knowing without doubt that I would hear tomorrow that filming at Glasgow cathedral had started. (That is just what happened.)

Near the car parking building I slipped in to a briskly efficient modern café and perched on a stool eating a pink cupcake and sipping a 'flat white'. From my angle upstairs I had plenty of opportunity to consider that in Glasgow I had seen more young men than any other city or town in Scotland, and in fact, it seemed the only city anywhere, where the number of men exceeded women by a good percentage.

By around 11am I was on the M77 driving south, heading towards the coast and a seaside town called Troon, notable to Outlanders as where Jamie, Claire and Murtagh arrive at the coast to board a ship for the Abbey in France. When I arrived at this coastline having travelled for 45 minutes on a four-lane road for the most part, it was a pleasure to find an almost empty beach that stretched into hazy distance. The beach was nice enough, but it was low tide, brown sand with bits of debris and driftwood, and cargo ships filling the horizon line where the hint of sea could be seen. Looking to my right I could see a tight row of old two-level attached houses toning in nicely with the sand and shore: this must be the township of Troon. At closer quarters, they were even quainter and I stopped the car and walked up and down the main street stretching my legs and investigating.

In deciding where I would go next, I had to choose between

a plethora of interesting spots, and there would be any number of castles between here and Wigtown, where I hoped to end up today. Dean Castle looked appealing and was not far from Troon, and looking back now on what I missed, I regret not taking the time. It boasts a woodland walk and 14th century castle in very good repair, which is from all accounts free to access.

However it was to Dundonald Castle that I made my way, driving increasingly narrow roads down country lanes, and seeing a small square castle on a hill by itself grow closer and closer. What convinced me to choose this one, was that it was a [19]"testimony, not only to the origins of the Royal Stewart dynasty, but also to the development of the nation of Scotland itself'. How could I drive past?

The castle is approached through the small village of Dundonald, and then up a lane which skirts a grassy hill that ends in a small car park and information centre/café. From there I walked up a short but steep path cresting the brow of the hill and beheld the ruins of the courtyard and compact little castle before me. All around in 360 degrees were the fields and townships of Ayrshire, disappearing into the hills in the distance. What a vantage point!

From what I read on the information leaflet, this castle had started life as a hill fort in the Dark Ages, belonging to a chieftain named Donald, hence Dun-Donald. Then Robert II in the 1370s built a castle in its place to mark his succession to the throne of Scotland. It has had a number of remodelling's over the centuries, mostly by the Stewarts, and although not a big castle, it commands a great view, and made a 'cosy' family fortification.

When I went in through the back entrance, into what would have been the cellars, I met an enthusiastic young lady wearing Dundonald Castle 'livery' and she spoke with passion about its history and layout. Above our heads was the most beautiful arched brick/stone ceiling, originally over the first floor hall, but lacking a floor between us, visible to the lower level. Apparently the space we

19. Dundonald Castle information brochure

stood in was hired out to wedding parties or small group functions, and I could see what a unique surround it would provide. I had the place to myself to roam around, and poked my head in through all the small doorways and windows, imagining the royal family entertaining a few guests in the hall upstairs, when it once had a roof, and tucking themselves to bed in the room above the dungeons.

Soon I felt the call to press on in my journey, and so I bade the helpful attendant farewell and set off down the slope to my car.

I continued on my journey south, bypassing Ayr, and (without knowing it) Robert Burn's Cottage, to see signs for Culzean Castle when I drove through Maybole township on the A71. Earlier in the day I had read that this castle was 'The Scottish National Trust's flagship property', and one of the most impressive of Scotland's great stately homes; I knew I could not forgo a visit. I learned that

– unlike many castles which were added to and remodelled over the years – Culzean was designed by Robert Adam in the 18th century, and so cleverly, that on approach it 'floats in to view like a mirage'. Naturally, I was agog to see such a thing.

The drive leading to this property is long and very promising, winding through forested park to end in front of the gate. A brick arched gateway framed the distant castle for my camera beautifully. Now, I cannot say that it looked like it was floating, but it bore all the features of a fairytale palace in pink-grey brick with tiny turrets, which is whimsical enough. After seeing the smaller Dundonald Castle earlier, with its ruined and more ancient walls, this one was at the other end of the spectrum. Set not on a hill, but on a cliff face, and in such beautifully manicured lawns and gardens, that they could hardly be compared. (Of course, it also depends what you are looking for in a castle!) Standing at the battlements overlooking the cliff and the vast ocean, Arran is in the hazy distance, and perhaps on a clear day, Ireland much further south. I chose not to pay the entrance fee to go in and look around this vastly larger castle, telling the two well-dressed young men in the entrance hall that I would just amble around the gardens instead. I love the inside of ancient castles, like Dundonald, but prefer the grounds of these more modern castles, and I was not disappointed. The sun was beating down outside (another reason to stay out and enjoy it), and the symmetrically designed front lawn with fountain and shrubs glowed rich green. There was a glasshouse open to view, the trees had their spring growth, various archways and bridges beckoned me to walk them, as well as a walled garden of topiary hedges, flowers and shrubs. It was lovely to bask outside with the sun on my face, enjoying the magnificent views all around.

I came out of my reverie, realising it was mid afternoon and time to keep rolling further south. After the turn off to Culzean, I drove across country on the A714, skirting the edges of Galloway Forest Park. When the sloping fields of countryside were not cleared

Left: Culzean Castle

for farming, small groves of trees clustered in low valleys or beside streams. The few townships I passed through were rich in blossom and wild hedges, and the road was often overhung with a thick border of trees. Apparently this Forest is a popular cycling area, and I longed to hire a bike and lose myself in the paths I glimpsed now and then. At Newton Stewart, the 'gateway to the Galloway Forest Park', which sits on the River Cree, a number of major roads converge. Avoiding the major roads, I continued on the A714 through Newton Stewart, and into progressively more farmed fields and hedgerows until the road passed a signpost stating, 'Scotland's National Book Town'. I had reached my destination: Wigtown.

Even had I not planned a night at this town, I would have, once I saw it. It resembled Beauly and a few other towns in that it had a triangular square with parking in the middle and a monument of some sort at the very centre. But Wigtown was quaint in other ways: every alternate stone store seemed to be a second hand bookshop, the ancient frontages were all beautifully preserved and eye-catching, and the town was not busy but had some 'life' about it. Of course, that could have been the effect of a sunny day on me in the last Scottish town I would stay in. I made a note of shops I would return to and crossed the road to the only B&B I could see, which just happened to be a café as well. One thing I had failed to do in my tweeting back and forth with Deborah, who owned Hillcrest House where I would be staying, was exchange phone numbers and find out the address! After my earlier successes in the

remote Scottish towns, where I stumbled upon my booked B&B by just turning up at the town, I assumed that the same would happen here.

The young woman who answered the door of the closed café/B&B on the main street, had not heard of my host's name, but the longer she talked the more she sounded familiar. It took me a moment, and her less, to realise we were both [20]Kiwis, and then with great glee, we proceeded down an ancient custom many will recognise:

Me: "Wait, where are ya from?"

Her: "I'm from Carterton! What about you?"

Me: "Sorry to say, I'm just another Aucklander. What are ya doing here of all places?"

Her: "Oh just doing some OE. I've been travelling for a few months now. Got a job at this café."

Me: "How long have you been here?" etc. etc.

The long and the short of it being that we were both equally delighted at hearing our own accent spoken and babbled away like we were long lost family. She was not able to help me with my

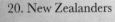
20. New Zealanders

search, so after promising to pop in the next day, I went back to the car and tweeted Deborah for directions. The response was not long in coming, and five minutes later I pulled in through the gate of an impressive old stone mansion with a beautiful archway leading up to the front door. This, then, was Hillcrest House.

Deborah Firth came out to meet me as I got out of the car, a beaming red-headed woman as short as I was tall. The two of us chattered merrily all the way in through the doors and up the wooden-bannistered staircase to a pretty pale blue room with two single beds in it and a high ceiling. A doorway on the side led to the blue and white bathroom. Not only do Deborah and her husband own this gorgeous guesthouse, but she is an accomplished cook, and they serve dinner and breakfast in the dining room if you book it. Best of all, she is an Outlander fan!

From my window I could see out over some rooftops to some wetlands and the sea, which my host informed me had a good walkway to a bird-watching hide, and also 'The Martyr's Stake.' (More on that later.)

Not having booked dinner with the Firths, I set off back up the road to the Town Centre, and parked outside The Wigtown Ploughman's Hotel. Inside, it was cosy and the filtered light from the summer evening shone through the front windows into the restaurant. I was very happy when given Old Mout cider from New Zealand, to read on the glass, 'take your tastebuds off road and discover a whole new world of cider from NZ. Get the kiwi taste for adventure.' Having just met another countrywoman on her own adventure, it was singularly appropriate.

After a hearty home-cooked meal, I drove down to the

car park beside the marshlands, and the path to the bird hide. Everything was lushly green and wet, the ponds and creeks swollen after the recent rainfall, and I was pleased to be dodging the muddy areas in the path in my Oban waterproof shoes. I passed a man in sturdy boots and coat, carrying his camera, who commented without any prompting from me: "There's nothing much, but I did see a couple of geese further out."

The boardwalk led up to a sturdy wooden hexagonal structure hanging out over a pond and the path. Inside, the walls had long slits for windows with wooden shutters that could be lifted or dropped to view the wildlife beyond. I perched on a bench and carefully levered one up, brushing away a few gnats that hovered near my face. For a long while it was perfectly still outside, although there were bird calls everywhere. A sudden flurry nearby and a small cloud of starlings (?) rose up and swept over the pool and away, too quick for my camera. The photo I took from the hide is bereft of any birds, but a favourite from my trip, it is so calm and redolent of lush green springtime.

When I had drunk my fill of the setting, and the midges were becoming a bother, I walked out to the car and drove up through the narrow single-lane road to Hillcrest House. There I lingered in the front parlour reading for a while, enjoying the deep burgundy armchairs and imagining the conversations that had happened beside that ornate fireplace. The last thing after a long

soak in the bath, was to stand at my window overlooking the bay, watching the light fade from pink to gold to mauve.

It was a beautiful last evening in Scotland.

Wednesday 10 June
Wigtown and away

It was with mixed feelings I descended the staircase to the spacious dining room for breakfast this morning; my last in Scotland.

On the one hand, since it had been such an Outlander-centred trip, it was great to be ending it with a new Outlander friend. On the other hand, I had so much I would have liked to yet see and experience, and what I had hoped to achieve in coming, had only served to whet my appetite for more.

The other guest sat nearby at his own table, and I had the impression was someone who was a regular guest at the house. He was a middle-aged man, very chatty and friendly, but I cannot now tell you what we talked of, my mind being preoccupied with the programme for my last day. I met Deborah's husband, who was our waiter, a man taller than I. Breakfast was efficiently delivered and delicious, and much too soon I was dragging my cases down from upstairs. One of the prizes that Deborah had won at the recent Outlander Gathering we both attended, was a life-size standee of Black Jack Randall, the villain in the series. She brought it out now, and I had a photo taken of Jack and I standing together, my face a complicated mixture of emotions, from sadness to fear, and not all because of the standee beside me. We parted warmly, and I set off to finish my investigation of Wigtown and its many attractions.

What I was most drawn to, out of all that Wigtown is famous for, was the 'Martyr's Stake' that I had heard about the day before. Having not found it when I walked around to the bird hide the previous evening, I determined to find it today. The story had been told me thus:

Back in 1600s at a time when Scottish Presbyterians took a 'covenant' to acknowledge Jesus Christ to be head of his church, being called 'Covenanters' for that reason, the Stuart Monarchs

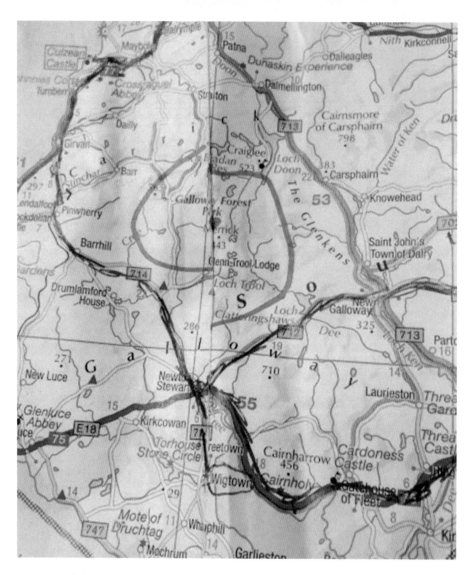

were claiming that the King had divine right to be head of the church. The resistance to the Stuarts was strong in this part of the country, and the powers-that-be in Wigtown decided to make an example of the oldest and youngest Covenanter women in the town, to stop the resistance spreading. On 11 May 1685, Margaret McLachlan aged 63, and Margaret Wilson, aged 18, were tied to stakes out in the tide, to recant or drown. The older woman was placed further out, so that her dying cries would cause the younger one to renege. They both drowned.

At the old church cemetery I found both their graves behind an iron fence, their names and epitaph chizeled by an ancient hand, and a focal point in the graveyard. Once I got past a [21]gravestone that amused me greatly, I reflected soberly on both the Margaret's fates.

Walking past the graveyard, a path leads down into the wetlands, with a marker pointing out the memorial Stake. At the point where the boardwalk out into the marsh begins, another modern notice stands with the full story of The Wigtown Martyrs. By the time I had walked out along the narrow boardwalk through reeds and swamp to the point where a concrete stake stands marking the place where they both drowned, I was very moved by what I had

seen and read. Here were two women who, for their beliefs alone, were cruelly drowned without ever surrendering their faith. After all my reading about the rise of Bonnie Prince Charlie, the Jacobite cause, which would put a Catholic King once more on the throne in Scotland, and the fateful battle at Culloden, it was a very sober reflection to know that there had been a great deal of injustice in general over the centuries. But somehow, these two ordinary village women, who partook in no war and were not soldiers, and yet were

21. 'A Tribute of Respect by members of the Total Abstinence Society' to Alexander Cowper who was 'Removed in the Midst of his Usefulness', a most 'consistent Christian.'

martyred for their faith, spoke to my heart most strongly. At the top of a hill overlooking the town is yet another striking memorial to the martyrs and the epitaph there finishes with a challenge to not surrender to tyranny:

... as a lesson to posterity never to lose or abuse those glorious privileges, planted by their labours, rooted in their suffering, and watered in their blood.

As I descended back into the town, it was gratifying to reflect that if they could see the outcome of their deaths all these years later, honoured in numerous ways around the town, (and those of their enemies completely forgotten), they might be greatly eased.

Before I left, I owed it to Wigtown to visit some of its many

bookshops, and the one that took my fancy was simply called 'The Book Shop – largest in Scotland'. From the outside it is significant only for the twin book pillars outside the door, but inside it was a different world entirely. The rooms went on and on, reflecting the theme of the books that jutted from the shelves below and around, the romance section had a bed suspended with red velvet cover; a fireplace had the quote: 'Give a man fire and he's warm for the day. But set fire to him and he's warm for the rest of his life.' (Terry Pratchett of course). There were curving stairways leading up to rooms above full of books, and when I thought I had come to the end of a corridor, lo and behold, another narrow passage led off into more chambers. It was the sort of place to spend a few hours easily, just browsing. As a parting souvenir it seemed appropriate to find a book to take with me, and I found two books that were perfect. The first was an old book from 1913, entitled 'The Contour Road

Book, Scotland – A Series of Elevation Plans of the Roads, with Measurements and Descriptive Letterpress' by Harry R. G. Inglis. After all my driving around Scotland, and particularly on many of the types of roads so well described by surveyors in this book, I enjoyed seeing the wild and wobbly line that indicated contours I had travelled. The second book was much more relevant though. 'Highland Journey' by Colin MacDonald was published in 1943 in Edinburgh, and I warmed to this man and his account of his life in the Highlands at the reading of his introduction:

'Let me be honest about this book-writing business. Why do I attempt it? For a great statesman, soldier, scientist. . . writing a book should be an easy matter and a safe venture for his publisher.

Such may rest assured of a public intensely interested in his sayings and doings. But that an ordinary fellow like myself should venture to write a book displays a degree of self-assurance, if not sheer impudence, which – because really I am somewhat of a modest disposition – requires some explanation.'

What followed on the pages was an account of Colin's early life from 1882 in a village of croft houses in the Highlands, through to his education and career as an agricultural spokesman for the government, cycling – yes, cycling – around those same Highlands to educate the locals on new developments. He went to the places I had visited, and he did it on a bicycle. I was hooked.

From that very day that I left Scotland, and began the rest of my holiday going down to Bournemouth and then Amsterdam, every night I read more of Colin's adventures, and on the last

day in the Netherlands before going home, I read the last page. It smoothed the transition out of my own Scottish adventure, and established me on the path to writing my own. (I was planning to anyway, but Mr MacDonald's own journey was a wonderful boost.)

I do not have much more to write of my Scottish adventure. By late morning I was driving out of Wigtown, on a brilliant blue day, heading across country on the A75 towards Carlisle. I had one major stop at Cairnholy, an hour from Wigtown. Not wanting to miss any major stone circles or burial cairns, I had been told about these the day before. I took the narrow steep track up in the car to the first cairn, which could be seen as a line of standing stones at the end of a grassy hummock. The hummock turned out to be an extensive burial chamber from the Neolithic period, extensively robbed over the course of time for field walls, but at the entrance is a line of about ten large stones. These form what must have been a ritual gathering place, and the two central stones look like a doorway. I was unable to squeeze through, which makes me feel that life was harder, shorter and people less - robust – 4000 to 6000 years ago. From their position on the hill, it was possible to see across a wide sweep of sea to what would be Wigtown way over on the far side. Standing in the same spot that humans have gathered for a length of time I cannot comprehend, is an amazing feeling, and I lingered for a while looking out at what they will have seen as well.

The second cairn, further up the hill, I could see was comprised of another burial mound and just a few standing stones. I reluctantly admit that I merely looked up there before returning to my car and the main road.

I pressed on towards Dumfries, stopping now and then for rest stops or refreshments, and at one point drove out of my way to try and see Threave Castle on an island in the River Dee. Here a boatman will row you across when you ring a bell. Feeling pressed for time, and seeing it involved a walk across the fields and woods, I satisfied myself with a sight of the turrets from the farm car park. When I return to Scotland, it is on my list of places to see.

Passing through the city of Carlisle, my attention riveted on the instructions from my I-phone, I failed to notice when I left Scotland and entered England. It was only as I pulled off the M6 at Penrith realising that I was no longer in the land of kilts and pipes, bannochs and haggis that I slumped behind the wheel in the service centre car park and let out a deep sigh.

I was heading out of the land in the books and series I love so much, away from the rugged mountains and deep lochs that so intrigue me, and into a different part of my journey, and finally, home.

Postscript

An unexpected delight occurred the day after I left Scotland.

Driving down toward Bournemouth that day, I skirted Wales and then cut across country to the south, avoiding London and Birmingham as much as I could. At one point, clutching the wheel and staring dully directly ahead on a smaller road cutting across flat grassy lands, I glanced to the right and almost swerved off the road. There, in all their magnificent granduer, were the standing stones of Stonehenge – starkly visible in the empty field. Smaller shapes, which were people, moved along the path beside them, but I soaked in the sight of that most well-known monument before it disappeared from view in my rear-vision mirror. I had paid to go up close and view these in my previous trip, and had many photos of that encounter. It seemed singularly appropriate to finish my travels with a glimpse of those stones as well.

Made in the USA
Lexington, KY
05 October 2015